Planning and Control of Municipal Revenues and Expenditures

By

Robert W. Ingram
University of Iowa

and

Ronald M. Copeland
Northeastern University

A study carried out on behalf of the
National Association of Accountants
New York, New York

Published by

National Association of Accountants
919 Third Ave., New York, N.Y. 10022

Charles Pridemore, Editor
Mandel & Wagreich, Inc., Cover

Copyright by National Association of Accountants © 1984. All rights reserved.
NAA Publication Number 83147
ISBN 0-86641-096-1

Foreword

All of us are concerned about the state of our nation's cities and other municipalities. Their financial conditions also are of professional concern to us as management accountants. It is a huge problem area which warrants our increased attention and active participation. We recognize it, in particular, as a problem which calls for more effective financial planning and control.

This report is designed to improve our understanding of municipal finances and to demonstrate the potential role of management accountants. The focus is on the proven means and techniques used commonly in business enterprises. The study demonstrates that they are applicable. It also exemplifies their application through descriptive case analyses.

Municipal revenue and expenditure patterns reflect a variety of socio-demographic and economic factors that affect both their revenue bases and service demands. Many of those factors were examined in the study, and 15 representative measures were selected to reflect three general dimensions: (a) income (five measures), (b) municipal economics (four measures) and (c) demographics (six measures).

Further examination of similarities and differences among cities enabled the researchers to identify four group patterns that are most meaningful for the purposes of financial planning and control. The resulting tables—shown in Chapter 3—are designed to serve for reference, as descriptive models, in preparing budgets and for performance evaluation.

The process employed in the study to identify group patterns and norms also lends itself readily to the city-specific data and norms. The relevant techniques and procedures are discussed in Chapter 4, and their application is illustrated in Chapter 5 by using actual data for six cities. Given the underlying differences among the cities, the six case analyses encompass a broad range of situations that are likely to be encountered in practice.

Guidance in the course of the research work and in the preparation of this report was generously and kindly provided by the Project Committee:

Milton F. Usry *(Chair)*
Oklahoma State University
Stillwater, Oklahoma

Homer R. Figler
CBN University
Virginia Beach, Virginia

Willard Cox
Oil City Iron Works
Corsicana, Texas

Theodore C. Gearhart
GAO-IRS
Washington, D.C.

The report reflects the views of the researchers and not necessarily those of the Association, the Committee on Research, or the Project Committee.

Stephen Landekich
Director of Research
National Association of Accountants

Acknowledgements

Numerous individuals contributed to this study. The Project Commitee provided constructive criticisms and helpful comments throughout the course of the study. In particular, Milton Usry provided prompt and effective guidance and was instrumental in the timely completion of the project. Stephen Landekich was most helpful in providing administrative and editorial support. The contributions of these individuals and others who provided technical and clerical assistance are gratefully acknowledged. Any remaining deficiencies are attibutable solely to the authors.

Robert W. Ingram
Ronald M. Copeland

Table of Contents

		Page
Foreword		iii
Acknowledgements		v
Chapter 1	— Planning and Control for Municipalities	1
Chapter 2	— Overview of Related Literature	7
Chapter 3	— Municipal Financial Patterns	15
Appendix A	— Municipal Financial Data	33
Appendix B	— Model Valuation	35
Chapter 4	— Budget and Cost Evaluation Procedures	39
Chapter 5	— Descriptive Analysis for Specific Cases	55
Appendix C	— Case C — Performance Evaluation	69
Appendix D	— Case D — Performance Evaluation	71
Appendix E	— Case E — Performance Evaluation	73
Appendix F	— Case F — Performance Evaluation	75
Selected Bibliography		77

List of Tables

Table Number		Page
3-1	Municipalities Grouped by Socio-Demographic Attributes	18
3-2	Linear Time Series Models for Total Revenue	21
3-3	Index of Change in Total Revenue, 1974-1979	22
3-4	Budget Items Included in Analysis	24-26
3-5	Description of Financial Variables	28
3-6	Average Annual Growth Rates for Financial Ratios	30
B-1	Descriptive Statistics for Holdout Sample	36
B-2	Statistics for Predictive Validity	37
4-1	Group Policy Budget for a Low Income, Low Growth City	41
4-2	City Projection Compared to Group Policy Budget	42
4-3	Comparison of City Projection to Flexible Group Norm Budget	44
4-4	Comparison of Actual with Projected Results	45
4-5	Comparison of Group and City Results	47
4-6	Program Costs and Budget Comparisons	49
4-7	Determination of Activity Level	50
4-8	Comparison of Budget with Cost at Actual Level of Activity	52
4-9	Fire Control Total Cost Variance Analysis	53
5-1	Case A — Budget Evaluation	57
5-2	Case A — Performance Evaluation	60
5-3	Case B — Budget Evaluation	61
5-4	Case B — Performance Evaluation	63
5-5	Case C — Budget Evaluation	64
5-6	Case D — Budget Evaluation	65
5-7	Case E — Budget Evaluation	66
5-8	Case F — Budget Evaluation	67

Planning and Control of
Municipal Revenues and Expenditures

Chapter 1

Planning and Control for Municipalities

Managerial planning and control of most business operations relies on accounting data. The information captured by business accounting systems reflects the acquisition of such input factors as labor, material, and overhead and their conversion into useful goods or services. Standard costs, flexible budgets, and forecasts are typical accounting tools which provide performance goals useful in making tactical decisions designed to improve enterprise efficiency or effectiveness.

On the other hand, local government managers may not use similar management accounting techniques because municipal[1] accounting systems are primarily designed to provide legal compliance information rather than information useful for planning and control purposes. Traditionally, municipal accounting systems are oriented toward the accumulation of financial accounting information rather than managerial accounting data. Municipal managers and professional organizations, however, are reevaluating this traditional role in light of the twin pressures for increased municipal services and reduced scope (cost) of government.

Another reason for the limited use of planning and control techniques in government is the lack of knowledge about the processes which link municipal costs and revenues, and knowledge about these linkages must underlie the development of rational forecasting and

---

[1] The term "municipality" generally is used in reference to a local government entity. In this study, the term will be used interchangeably with "city" because the empirical data are limited to cities. Similar applications of management control procedures could apply to counties, school districts, or special service districts.

evaluation procedures. While business costs and revenues are responsive to the underlying production, sales, and investment processes, municipal costs and revenues are not subject to the same discipline of the free enterprise system. Municipal cost and revenue generating processes are more independent of each other and reflect complex social, legal, and economic circumstances. Prospects for improvement in municipal planning and control procedures depend upon a better understanding of the forces which control the supply of municipal input factors and the demand for municipal services.

The objectives of this study are: 1. to summarize relevant municipal planning and control literature, 2. to examine the feasibility of applying commonly used business sector management planning and control techniques to municipalities, 3. to illustrate a straightforward, practical method of application based on actual municipal financial data, 4. to evaluate the potential validity of the application and 5. to apply the methods to actual cases to illustrate their usefulness for planning and control purposes.

Overview of Research Method

The data bases underlying the empirical portion of this project cover approximately 1,400 cities with populations in excess of 10,000 drawn from all geographical areas.

The research methodology consisted of six phases.

Phase 1:

Professional literature concerned with the supply of and demand for municipal goods and services was analyzed. A bibliography of potentially relevant literature was developed and the literature was examined to identify previous studies of cost and revenue behavior.

Phase 2:

Sociological, demographic, and economic attributes that potentially determine municipal revenue and expenditure patterns were examined. A computerized municipal data base provided variables that represent socio-demographic and economic attributes for a large cross section of municipalities. The data base contains information on most U.S. cities with populations in excess of 10,000. After examining descriptive characteristics of the variables and relationships among the variables, cluster analysis[2] was used to differentiate groups of cities, so that each group consisted of cities having similar socio-demographic and economic attributes. A profile for each group of cities was developed.

Phase 3:

A computerized municipal financial data base provided revenues and expenditures for 1973-1979 for all cities in each Phase 2 group. Next, revenue and expenditure patterns for each group were identified, along with statistics on the reliability of the models, and differences between groups were examined. This allowed the stability of the patterns over time to be determined for 1973-1979.

Phase 4:

Revenue and expenditure patterns were validated by comparing the original patterns to a sample of cities that were not included in the original analysis. The socio-demographic and economic attributes of each city in the "validating" sample were examined, and the cities were assigned to one of the experimental groups as in Phase 2 above. Using models developed in Phase 3, the expected revenue values and expenditure patterns for each city were forecasted. The forecast error was measured by comparing the actual and estimated values for each variable.

Phase 5:

The use of the revenue and expenditure pattern models in planning and controlling municipal finances was described. Expenditure and revenue standards were developed. The standards were combined with flexible budgeting techniques to describe forecast and variance analysis procedures that can be employed by municipal managers.

---

[2]Cluster analysis is a statistical technique for grouping observations based on similarities and differences in various attributes of the observations. Observations that are most similar are clustered into common groups.

Phase 6:

Individual cases that apply the Phase 5 procedures were selected to illustrate different aspects of the management accounting techniques and to demonstrate their utility.

Potential Benefits of the Study

Municipal financial management personnel, business managers, and municipal constituents have traditionally viewed accounting predominantly from a legal compliance, external control perspective. Frequently, municipal financial managers do not interact with other managerial personnel who perceive a broad and significant role for accounting as a management decision tool. Increased interaction and cooperation between private and public managers could be mutually beneficial through increased interaction and involvement by municipal management.

Planning and controlling municipal finances is not only a concern of public managers. Private business is affected by municipal financial performance because it is a prime source of municipal revenues and a recipient of municipal services. Planning for plant location or expansion, planning for new investment and employee satisfaction, and planning for long-run profitability all depend to some extent on awareness of municipalities' financial conditions and expected performances. Such research can be useful to private business as a tool for decision making, and the techniques we have proposed, along with the data base used, can provide business managers a means for estimating future municipal performance and for evaluating actual performance.

The financial crises faced by many of our nation's cities perhaps could have been avoided if more attention had been given earlier to effective financial planning and control. Improving financial conditions and preventing future crises requires the involvement of municipal constituents who as voters have the power to alter municipal economic behavior. Constituents may improve municipal financial conditions by assisting in making public managers aware of their insistence on the use of appropriate techniques for planning and control.

Summary of Findings

The empirical results of this study reveal that municipalities can be classified into socio-demographic groups. Four distinct groups of cities were identified that could be characterized according to two dimensions: high and low per capita income and high and low percentage change (growth) in per capita income. These groups provide a basis for examining revenues and expenditures because cities with similar environmental constraints (socio-demographic attributes) should experience similar resource needs and service demands.

In order to compare financial patterns, a common denominator was identified to control for differences in size across cities and in the purchasing power of the dollar across time. Total revenue was selected as a useful base for computing financial ratios because of conceptual and empirical characteristics described in the study.

Twenty-one revenue and expenditure ratios were calculated for two samples of 390 cities each using total revenue as the denominator. These ratios appeared to be relatively stable over the 1973 to 1979 period within socio-demographic groups. Noticeable differences were observed across groups for most ratios. The ratios were found to be stable within groups and across time periods, facilitating planning and control decisions. Very similar results were found within each of the two independent samples. Thus, these results indicate that by identifying the socio-demographic group to which a city belongs, one can project revenues and expenditures as a percent of total revenue fairly accurately for most cities, and based on these projections, planning and control decisions can be made.

Planning or budgeting decisions can be aided by reference to group norms. Knowledge of the actual or expected revenues and expenditures of cities with similar environmental constraints provides a basis for projecting the revenues and expenditures of an individual city. The relation between actual and planned performance provides a basis for assessing the causes of variances and for modifying performance where it is necessary and can be controlled.

The financial ratios for each group also can provide a basis for evaluating revenues and expenditures at different levels of operations. Group norms and flexible budgeting techniques can help a city project revenues and expenditures at different levels of total revenue. Given the most recent economic recession, such planning can be useful for avoiding fiscal crises or at least for taking early steps to deal with these problems. Flexible budgets also provide a standard for comparison of actual results when these results differ from budget because the total revenue base was different from expected.

Cases for six cities using actual financial data are illustrated. Comparisons are made between planned revenues and expenditures and group norms and between actual revenue and expenditures and group norms. These comparisons reveal policy choices made by city managers concerning the incidence of social costs and the allocation of public resources. Analysis of these results also reveals management effectiveness in the use of resources relative to cities in the same socio-demographic and economic environments. The analysis suggests that financial problems arise from how a city responds to resource constraints.

Chapter 2
Overview of Related Literature

An abundance of literature on municipal forecasting, budgeting and related topics has been produced in the last few years. This study differs from these earlier studies in three respects: it examines a larger cross section of cities, hence it can support broader generalizations about the total sample as well as across subgroups in the sample, and generalizations are related to managerial decisions.

Most works on this subject can be classified into several categories according to the major focus or purpose of each study: 1. state of the art surveys, 2. manuals identifying the use of specific tools or procedures in a given location, 3. practical guides to the use of financial management tools, 4. case studies of financial management problems or evaluations, 5. theoretical examinations of what determines financial policies, 6. empirical studies of factors influencing financial events. These categories are not necessarily mutually exclusive.

State of the Art Surveys

A prime example of this category is *Multi-Year Revenue and Expenditure Forecasting* (U.S. Department of Housing and Urban Development, 1980). This manual was a product of the Financial Management Capacity Sharing Program that was intended to provide federal assistance for local government financial management problems. The document underscores the need for intermediate-range financial planning and evaluation.

The survey of current practices found that few cities (less than 16% of cities with populations larger than 250,000) employ multiple year forecasts. They use a variety of techniques including expert judgment, trend analysis, and statistical and econometric models. These approaches are discussed and illustrated by reference to their use in individual cities. The bulk of the publication consists of descriptions of forecasting practices in Dallas, New Orleans, New York, Portland, San Antonio, and Washington, D.C.

Another example of this type of study is "Forecasting Local Government Budgets" by Roy Bahl and Larry Schroeder (Syracuse University, Maxwell School of Public Affairs, 1979). This study also surveys a number of cities and evaluates the various methods used. It provides detailed descriptions of the individual cities' practices. Cities used in the study include New York, New Orleans, San Diego, Dallas, and San Antonio.

The studies in this category indicate the benefits and costs of specific techniques as they are employed in particular communities. They are limited, however, because of the small group of selected cities used in the analyses. In contrast, a primary objective of our study is to identify general methods and forecasting models that can be adapted to a variety of individual locations. The studies represented in this category provide the present research with descriptions of models and variables that may have general application. They also provide a standard against which the results of this research can be compared.

This literature characterizes municipal governments as having many attributes that also are found in labor-intensive functions of mature business organizations. Thus, it is possible to draw on financial management tools used by business to enhance the planning and control functions in local governments. Using these tools requires an understanding of the government fiscal and behavioral environment. One task of our study is to develop a forecasting system that will be applicable to specific needs within the municipal environment.

A different type of survey is represented by *Trends in the Fiscal Condition of Cities: 1978–1980* (Government Printing Office, 1980). The federal government frequently surveys states and municipalities to identify fiscal problems and potential contributions of federal policies. This study identifies changing revenue and expenditure patterns and concludes that an increasing number of cities will face fiscal strain during the 1980s.

Manuals Describing Municipal Practices

Municipalities that have adopted formal financial forecasting procedures frequently publish manuals describing their practices. These documents vary considerably in detail and coverage. Some are little more than advertisements describing the benefits of the city's financial management procedures. Others are detailed explanations of the model, variables, and assumptions used to forecast revenues and expenditures.

An example of the latter type of manual is that published by the City of New Orleans, *Municipal Budget Projections* (1977). This manual also identifies the background from which the forecasting procedures were developed and traces the steps that led to the adoption of the procedures.

Practical Guides to Financial Management Practices

A variety of "how to" publications are available for anyone interested in municipal financial forecasting and budgeting. Some of these guides provide a thorough analysis of the issues and concepts of financial forecasting. They suggest specific techniques and variables that may be used to project financial performance or fiscal strain. Unfortunately, they are seldom based on a rigorous theoretical or empirical foundation. Instead, they rely on personal insights and anecdotal observations to link a variety of factors to revenues and expenditures.

A typical example in this category is *Economic Analysis for Local Government* (National League of Cities, 1977). This publication looks at a series of financial problems that a city may face and offers methods for dealing with the problems. Issues dealt with in the document include: understanding a city's economic base, labor market analysis, revenue projections, cost-benefit analysis, pricing user charges, and monetary flow analysis. The publication thoroughly discusses each issue, suggests measurement techniques, and provides worksheets for calculating indices for a specific municipality.

A similar publication is *Is Your City Heading for Financial Difficulty?* (Municipal Finance Officers Association, 1978). This document also presents a selection of techniques that may be used to analyze a municipality's financial condition. The techniques are presented in a series of sequential steps to assist a manager in making calculations and interpreting results.

Conditions discussed in the document include: decline in economic vitality, loss of financial independence and flexibility, declining productivity, deferral of costs, and unsound financial management practices. Trend analysis is the method suggested for evaluating financial condition. Numerous ratios are described that may be used in the time-series models; however, standards for comparing the trends are not provided.

Another publication illustrative of this category is *Municipal Fiscal Indicators* (U.S. Department of Housing and Urban Development, 1980). Like the previous document, this guide examines forecasting techniques for prediction of fiscal strain. It defines fiscal indicators and describes how to use them. This study also summarizes a number of projects that have attempted to identify and employ fiscal indicators.

A number of journal articles have been written that describe financial forecasting methods. "Local Government Expenditure Forecasting" by Robert Cramer (*Governmental Finance*, November 1978) discusses a number of practical issues involved in forecasting. Illustrations of forecasts and the steps involved also are provided.

"Financial Indicators" by Sanford Groves, et al. (*Public Budgeting and Finance*, Spring 1981), provides a systematic approach to financial indicator analysis. The indicators are integrated into an interactive system of related measures. In addition, the system has been tested in a small sample of municipalities with good results.

Case Studies

Publications in this category consist of applications of forecasting methodology to a single or a small group of municipalities. The advantages of this approach are in permitting an extensive examination of the specific factors affecting a given location. A large amount of data, some of which may not be available for a large number of cities, may be examined intensively. The disadvantage is that the results are not generalizable to other municipalities and the models used generally cannot be used to develop cross-sectional comparisons because the models are specifically related to a given location.

An example of this type of study is "Municipal Finances in Perspective: A Look at Interjurisdictional Spending and Revenue Patterns" by Elizabeth Hansen (*Journal of Accounting Research*, Supplement, 1977). This study examines financial conditions in Rochester, Buffalo, and Syracuse, New York. Comparisons are made in revenue and expenditure patterns after controlling for population size. The efficiency of municipal operations, debt position, and financial strain indicators are examined across cities as a basis for predicting future financial performance.

Another example in this category is "Forecasting the Local Government Budget" by Roy Bahl, et al., (*National Tax Association Proceedings*, November 1977). This study develops a forecasting model and applies it to Syracuse, New York.

Theoretical Studies

A major theory to explain differences in municipal expenditure patterns is presented by Charles Tiebout in "A Pure Theory of Local Expenditures," *Journal of Political Economy* (October 1956). Tiebout's theory assumes that individuals move freely among political jurisdictions. Cities will attempt to attract desirable constituents (individuals and businesses) while attempting to discourage undesirables by offering a package of goods and services that appeals to the desirables but not the undesirables.

Tiebout's theory is important for the current study since it asserts that municipalities differ as to the optimal pattern of revenues and expenditures. Different groups of cities must be examined for common economic and socio-demographic characteristics before meaningful revenue and expenditure projections can be made.

Werner Hirsch, in *The Economics of State and Local Governments* (McGraw-Hill, 1970), examines the nature of municipal cost functions. Economies of scale are a major consideration in private sector production. Municipal services, however, do not lend themselves well to such scale economies. Most services are capital intensive, and as a city grows or as consolidation occurs, it generally must create additional facilities in different locations to provide improved service. As a result, average cost functions for many municipal services are relatively flat. Thus, the average cost of providing services does not change substantially as the quantity of services increases. This concept reduces the complexity of municipal forecasting since cost normally will be proportional to the quantity of services provided. The major exception is in the area of enterprise operations which generally follow a private sector, declining average cost process.

Anthony Downs, in *An Economic Theory of Democracy* (Harper, 1957), hypothesizes that revenue and expenditure patterns are strongly influenced by a politician's desire to remain in office. Accordingly, a budget is designed with reference to a specific constituency in an attempt to satisfy the needs of a dominant coalition of voters. Thus, different municipalities will probably have similar revenue and expenditure patterns only if they have populations with similar economic and socio-demographic characteristics.

Empirical Studies

Numerous articles have been written that attempt to identify the factors which determine municipal revenue and expenditure patterns by examining actual sample data. Some of these studies rely on or test theories which predict the patterns such as the theories of Tiebout and Downs. More frequently, the studies adopt an ad hoc model or test the influence of a specific factor on municipal revenues or expenditures. The studies can be divided to four subcategories into which the empirical literature can be classified: tests of the Tiebout theory, tests of the Downsian theory, studies of fiscal stress, and mathematical models of specific financial determinants.

Tests of the Tiebout Theory

J. Richard Aronson and Eli Schwartz, in "Financing Public Goods and the Distribution of Population in a System of Local Governments" (*National Tax Journal,* June 1973), developed a model of population migration based on differences in financial performance across municipalities. Forecasts were derived to predict the relative change in municipal populations. Population changes in the towns in the Harrisburg, Pa., area were tested, and a significant portion of the population shifts were predicted correctly. The model was based on the difference between the benefits derived from local expenditures and the costs to constituents of local taxes. Individuals were hypothesized to attempt to maximize their net benefits.

This study is important in that it stresses the link between financial performance and population movement. As populations shift, the economic base and service demands of a location also change. Forecasting future revenue and expenditure patterns requires an understanding of these population shifts.

In "Residential Choice and the Local Public Sector: An Alternative Test of the 'Tiebout Hypothesis'" (*Journal of Urban Economics*, 1979), Andrew Reschovsky, by using data from the Minneapolis-St. Paul, Minn., area, found that local revenue and expenditure factors influenced residential choice decisions. Furthermore, the effects were different across different economic classes. Thus, a local government can potentially alter the socio-economic composition of its citizens and the size of its economic base.

Tests of Downsian Theory

Otto Davis and George Haines, in "A Political Approach to a Theory of Public Expenditure: The Case of Municipalities" (*National Tax Journal,* September 1966), confirms that the socio-demographic composition of a municipality is an important factor influencing the pattern of local expenditures. Data on towns in the Pittsburgh, Pa., area were used to demonstrate the differences in service mixes associated with different population mixes. Composition is thus an important consideration in forecasting municipal revenues and expenditures.

A similar study by Thomas Borcherding and Robert Deacon, "The Demand for the Services of Non-Federal Governments" (*The American Economic Review,* December 1972), provides a more detailed mathematical formulation of the model and a more rigorous test. It produces results consistent with those of Davis and Haines. State rather than municipal data were used.

Studies of Fiscal Stress

"Fiscal Management of American Cities: Funds Flow Indicators" by Terry Clark (*Journal of Accounting Research,* Supplement, 1977) considered a number of financial measures to evaluate potential deficits in a a group of 51 cities. The study found a significant relationship between certain financial characteristics and indices of fiscal stress.

In "Understanding Central City Hardship," Richard Nathan and Charles Adams (*Political Science Quarterly,* Spring 1976) explain the development of a stress index that is used to rank 66 large cities. Several socio-economic factors are identified that relate to fiscal stress.

Studies of Specific Determinants of Financial Performance

In "Factors Associated with Variations in State and Local Government Spending" (*Journal of Finance,* September 1966), Roy Bahl and Robert Saunders measure the association between per capita expenditures of governmental units and a variety of explanatory variables such as income, density, and federal grants. Changes in the models over time also are evaluated.

"The Differential Impact of Manufacturing and Mercantile Activity on Local Government Expenditures and Revenues" by Douglas Booth (*National Tax Journal,* March 1978) examines the effect of differences in a city's business activity on its financial performance. The study points out the importance of economic attributes for explaining revenue and expenditure patterns.

Implications for the Current Research

This study attempts to integrate the theoretical and empirical considerations of previous studies into a research design that can be applied to a large sample of municipalities. The research fits best into the empirical studies category and extends work into empirical tests of theoretical models of determinants of revenue and expenditure patterns. In addition, the factors that were identified by previous studies as having a significant effect on municipal revenues and expenditures are examined on a larger scale.

The focus of our study differs from previous research, however, in that generalizable models are developed and validated that may be applied to a large segment of cities. The large sample analysis also permits validation of the models by application of the same procedures to independent samples. Results can then be compared across samples. In addition, the models can be examined for stability over time. Thus, an improvement is offered over previous research in terms of sample size. Primary among these advantages is the ability to control for differences in the demographic and economic bases of municipalities that is not possible with small samples.

Chapter 3

Municipal Financial Patterns

At any point in time, observers may identify key attributes of a city's infrastructure, population, or environmental endowment that determine most of its financial characteristics. These variables may be referred to as socio-demographic attributes. Furthermore, in a large sample of cities, those with similar attributes can be grouped into subsamples of similar cities. The financial patterns of cities within a subsample will be similar to the extent that the socio-demographic attributes used in classifying cities actually do capture underlying revenue and expenditure generating processes.

Because the incidences of costs and benefits of public goods frequently are not uniform, municipal financial characteristics may change over time as different coalitions desiring different service patterns become dominant in given locations. Thus, both the current magnitude of socio-demographic attributes and the direction of change in these attributes are potential factors affecting financial patterns. The patterns may be expected to differ depending on the current mix of constituents that affect service demands and revenue bases. The patterns may shift over time as the mix changes. Predicting future revenues and expenditures depends on expected shifts in the mix.

Selection of Attributes

The particular socio-demographic attributes of importance for identifying service demands and revenue bases are a subject for empirical analysis. Previous research has examined a variety of measures, including: population change (Ladd, 1980), density, personal income (Ohls and Wales, 1972), magnitude and variety of business activity (Booth, 1977), and population demographics (Borcherding and Deacon, 1972). These and other studies have shown that sociodemographics are useful predictors of municipal expenditures.

In our study, a number of representative factors were selected for examination. The selection was based on two criteria: reference to previous studies such as those described above and available data for a large cross section of municipalities.[1] Data were available for 780 cities, and these cities constitute our total sample.

Fifteen socio-demographic variables for fiscal 1972 and 1977 (the years closest to the fiscal periods studied) were selected to represent various dimensions of the cities' endowments. Both static and dynamic attributes were selected to reflect both the magnitude and changes in magnitude of the variables. The 15 variables reflect three general dimensions: income, municipal economics, and city demographics.

Five measures of income are: per capita personal income, median family income, per capita business income, percentage change in per capita personal income, and percentage change in per capita business income. Four measures of municipal economics are: unemployment (percentage), percentage of total population below poverty level, business diversification index [2], and percentage of total housing currently occupied. Six measures of city demographics are: area (square miles), population density, percentage of nonwhite population, percentage of population over age 64, birth rate, and percentage change in total population.

The interrelationships among these variables were examined to determine the number of distinct factors that should be considered in identifying similar cities. A correlation matrix revealed that all of the factors except the percentage change factors were intercorrelated at the .05 probability level. The percentage change factors also were intercorrelated among themselves at the .05 level.

The magnitude of the intercorrelations suggests that the sensitivity in selection of attributes for grouping cities is relatively low; i.e., one attribute can be substituted for another. Certain patterns of attributes pertain to most municipalities. For example, a low personal income city also generally has low levels of business income

---

[1]The latter criterion was implemented by reference to the *City-County Data Book* (CCDB) published in five-year intervals by the U.S. Department of Commerce, Bureau of Census. These data were selected because they contain a detailed description of the social, demographic, and economic attributes of municipalities larger than 50,000 population. The data and sample are as comprehensive as any available.

The set of cities contained in the CCDB was matched against cities for which financial data were available as described in footnote 7.

[2]The Index was computed to reflect the balance of business activity from the retail, wholesale manufacturing, and service segments.

and activity, high levels of unemployment and poverty, high density, and high percentages of nonwhite and elderly population. These correlations are logical and explain the similarity of results of previous studies that have employed different variables. The choice of variables does not appear to be critical.

On the other hand, the distinction between static and dynamic dimensions does appear to be important. Cities with different static attributes (e.g., low income versus high income) do not necessarily share the same dynamic attributes (e.g., low growth in income). One low income city may be growing and increasing its income level while another may be declining.

Identification of Classes

The socio-demographic variables were used to group the cities into relatively homogeneous classes. A clustering algorithm was used that separates observations by statistical measures of similarity and difference.[3]

Then, several combinations of variables were examined; however, two variables appeared to be as useful for separating the sample into statistically different groups as any other combination. These variables were per capita personal income and percentage change in per capita personal income. Given the intercorrelations among the variables, it is logical that two attributes representing static and dynamic dimensions would measure most of the differences across the cities. In addition, these two variables have conceptual appeal for this study. Logical differences exist between the service demands and revenue bases of high versus low income cities.

Four distinct groups were derived from the cluster analysis. Descriptive statistics for these groups are shown in Table 3-1.[4] The grouping represents four classes of municipalities: low income, low growth — Group 1, high income, low growth — Group 2, low income, high growth — Group 3, and high income, high growth — Group 4. Thus, different service demands and revenue bases, and changes therein, are characterized by these groups. These four patterns of socio-demographic characteristics should be useful for pro-

---

[3]F ratios were calculated to determine whether the groups were statistically different and to determine which variables were useful for differentiating among the observations.

[4]The groups were significantly different for the per capita income and percentage change in income variables at the .05 level.

TABLE 3-1

Municipalities Grouped by Socio-Demographic Attributes

Variable	Group 1 (N = 262) Mean	Std.	Group 2 (N = 152) Mean	Std.	Group 3 (N = 236) Mean	Std.	Group 4 (N = 130) Mean	Std.
Income:								
Per capita	4255	413	6002	1270	4220	454	5627	790
Family	9648	1122	12850	2439	8625	1284	11482	2157
Business	8650	4150	10550	8270	8050	3630	9190	5990
Change in per capita	.40	.04	.40	.05	.53	.05	.53	.08
Change in business	.19	1.06	.18	.75	.30	1.62	.74	1.72
Economic:								
Percent unemployment	.05	.02	.04	.01	.05	.02	.04	.01
Percent below poverty	.12	.05	.06	.03	.16	.07	.08	.04
Business diversification	.24	.05	.26	.05	.26	.05	.26	.06
Percent occupied housing	.95	.02	.97	.02	.94	.02	.96	.02
Demographic:								
Area	23.9	32.7	21.8	47.0	43.3	83.9	28.4	35.3
Density	5106	4549	5896	3514	2798	1574	3916	2389
Percent nonwhite	.10	.13	.06	.09	.16	.15	.07	.09
Percent over 65	.11	.03	.10	.04	.10	.03	.09	.06
Birth rate	.02	.00	.01	.00	.02	.00	.01	.00
Population growth rate	.00	.07	.01	.06	.05	.10	.05	.09

N = number of observations
Std. = standard deviation

jecting changing patterns of municipal revenues and expenditures.[5]

The partitioning of cities provides a framework for the analysis which follows in the next chapter. Financial patterns will differ across these groups and will be similar within groups if the partitioning has captured attributes that affect service demand and revenue base attributes. The clustering procedure appears to have separated the total sample into relatively homogeneous (significantly different) classes.

It may be useful to visualize the classes in a diagram:

	Low Growth	High Growth
High Income	Group 2	Group 4
Low Income	Group 1	Group 3

High income cities are expected to have larger and more diverse revenue bases than low income cities and to demonstrate different levels of expenditure for various services. Cities that have growing revenue bases should be more financially stable and should be expanding primary services in comparison to cities with declining bases. This will be evident as we examine these differences across the classes of municipalities in an attempt to model the financial patterns and provide comparative standards for evaluating resource management.

Modeling Financial Performance

Different budget orientations can control municipal budgeting decisions. There are two types of municipal budgeting: revenues are first estimated, and then the total amount is allocated to satisfy the expenditure needs; and expenditures are first estimated on the basis of expected needs, and then tax rates and other revenue elements are specified at levels to satisfy these needs. Obviously, some degree of interaction occurs in most municipal budgeting operations. We have selected total revenue as the dominant budget variable.

---

[5]The use of only four groups in the empirical analysis is a simplification of the real world environment. A tradeoff is being made between ease of manipulation and description from using four groups on one hand and precision on the other. The significant differences among the groups, however, suggest that the amount of precision lost by using these groups is not large.

Total revenue is a conceptually appealing base because it represents the resources available for budgeting. Using total revenue as a base is similar to preparing common size income statements for business in that each element of revenue and expenditure is represented by its percentage of the total budget, the importance of each constituent element can be assessed, and cross-sectional and time series comparisons are facilitated. Also, using total revenue as a base controls for price level changes.[6]

The linear time series models for each of the four groups of cities is shown in Table 3-2. Growth in personal income is associated with the growth in revenue over the period tested. The low income, high growth group exhibited the largest increase in total revenue. The low income, low growth group exhibited the smallest increase in total revenue. These models all have high explanatory power which indicates that the revenue for next year can readily be estimated on the basis of revenue of the current year.

The relative changes in total revenue for each group are described in Table 3-3. Relative changes were measured by comparing the magnitude of total revenue each year from 1974-1979 with the magnitude in 1973. Thus, an index was formed in which 1973 = 100. Table 3-3 indicates that the changes in total revenue for the low growth groups (Group 1 and 2) were lower throughout the period than the high growth groups. These patterns are similar to those in Table 3-2. Total revenue increased throughout the period for all groups (Table 3-3).

Linear extrapolation of total revenue for predicting the level of future revenues is relatively straightforward. Over the seven years examined, the total revenue patterns for each group were relatively linear. This means that simple extrapolation of prior years' observations is appropriate for budgeting purposes.

Municipal budgets usually disclose financial estimates for several classes of revenue and expenditure elements. Our selection of these elements was dictated by the accounting practices common to a

---

[6]Another important reason for using total revenue as a base is its statistical properties. The distributions and growth rates of various financial numbers were examined. Total revenue is one of the most stable and predictable municipal numbers. Over the 1978-1979 period, total revenue for the sample of 780 cities studied remained approximately constant on a per capita basis. In addition, the average coefficient of determination (R^2— a measure of linearity) for the first-order time series (revenue in t = revenue in period t − 1) was approximately .75.

TABLE 3-2

Linear Time Series Models for Total Revenue*

Group	Model Parameters
Group 1 — Low Income, Low Growth	$TR_t = .01 + .91\ TR_{t-1}$, $R^2 = .68$
Group 2 — High Income, Low Growth	$TR_t = .03 + .95\ TR_{t-1}$, $R^2 = .77$
Group 3 — Low Income, High Growth	$TR_t = .02 + 1.18\ TR_{t-1}$, $R^2 = .75$
Group 4 — High income, High Growth	$TR_t = .01 + 1.02\ TR_{t-1}$, $R^2 = .75$

*Revenue was expressed in thousands.

TABLE 3-3

Index of Change in Total Revenue, 1974–1979
1973 = 100

Year	Group 1 Mean	Group 1 Std.	Group 2 Mean	Group 2 Std.	Group 3 Mean	Group 3 Std.	Group 4 Mean	Group 4 Std.
1974	114	138	111	127	122	214	114	126
1975	121	162	121	151	136	263	128	188
1976	135	199	133	206	155	362	147	361
1977	144	272	144	253	168	457	161	434
1978	163	487	167	501	192	512	187	538
1979	178	440	176	426	216	602	202	633

large sample of cities and by the availability of data.[7] A standard set of revenue and expenditure categories was designed to provide useful data that are representative of the categories found in the financial statements of most municipalities.[8] Certain budget items are reported by many cities, and 21 were selected for analysis in this study (Table 3-4).

Also, financial ratios can be used when making fiscal comparisons across cities with different populations or across time. In these types of comparisons, financial data must be standardized to control for intervening variables, such as changes in population. Because we consider financial data for 780 cities over several periods, we standardized our financial data by dividing each budget item by the total revenue base to create a ratio.[9] Thus, ratios indicate the percentage of total revenue used to provide various services.

Description of Financial Patterns

The sample of 780 cities was randomly divided into two subsamples of 390. One subsample was used to validate the models, as described in Appendix B to this chapter. Descriptive statistics for each ratio for 1973 and 1979 (the beginning and end of the period

---

[7]The most comprehensive data source for municipal financial data is *City Government Finances* prepared annually by the Bureau of the Census. Data are collected on over 1,500 cities and are reported in standardized format including revenue sources and expenditure functions. These data were cross matched with the *City-County Data Book* to produce the sample included in this study.

Data from *City Government Finances* have been aggregated into primary revenue and expenditure categories and have been reformatted into a time series by the authors for research purposes. A summary description of the data is provided in Appendix A to this chapter. For further discussion see Ingram and Copeland (1981).

[8]The current analysis is limited to these categories and does not include special funds or budget categories that may differ considerably across cities.

[9]Population is frequently used to reduce municipal financial data to a common base. Several problems may be created by this process. In this study, population and growth were used in classifying municipalities into homogeneous classes. Per capita financial data might confound the results by introducing the same variable into the financial pattern analysis. More importantly, per capita numbers are not always comparable since the level of expenditure is not necessarily a linear function of population. In addition, per capita ratio involves the use of a exogenous, nonfinancial variable, rather than a decision variable from within the financial planning process.

In this study, we chose to test the usefulness of the financial base itself as a comparative measure. To be useful, the base should be relatively stable or should change uniformly over time and should reflect a basic financial dimension of municipalities.

TABLE 3-4

Budget Items Included in Analysis

Item	Definition
Property Tax (PTAX)	Taxes conditioned on ownership of property and measured by its value.
Total Own Revenue (OWNR)	All amounts of money received by a government from external sources other than from issuance of debt, liquidation of investments, as agency and private trust transactions.
Total Outside Revenue (OUTR)	Amounts received from other governments as fiscal aid in the form of shared revenues and grants-in-aid, as reimbursements for performance of general government functions and specific services for the paying government.
Education Expenditure (EDUC)	Schools and other educational facilities and services.
Financial Administration Expenditures (FADM)	Municipal officials and agencies concerned with tax assessment and collection, accounting, auditing, budgeting, purchasing, custody of funds, and other central finance activities.
Fire Protection Expenditures (FIRE)	City fire fighting organization and auxiliary services inspection for fire hazards, and other fire prevention activities.
General Control Expenditures (GCON)	The governing body, municipal courts, office of the chief executive, and central staff services and agencies.
Health and Hospital Expenditures (HOSP)	Health services including health research, clinics, nursing, immunization, and other categorical, environmental, and general public health activities. Establishment and operation of hospital facilities, provision of hospital care, and support of other public or of private hospitals.

TABLE 3-4 (continued)

Item	Definition
Highways and Streets Expenditures (HIGH)	Streets, highways, and structures necessary for their use, snow and ice removal, toll highway and bridge facilities, and ferries.
Housing Expenditures (HOUS)	City housing and redevelopment projects and regulation, promotion, and support of private housing and redevelopment activities.
Interest Expenditures (INTR)	Interest payments except for utility debt.
Parking Expenditures (PARK)	Municipal public-use garages and other parking facilities operated on a charge basis.
Parks and Recreation Expenditures (RECR)	Cultural-scientific activities, such as museums and art galleries; organized recreation, including playgrounds and play fields, swimming pools and bathing beaches; municipal parks; and special facilities for recreation.
Police Expenditures (POLC)	Preservation of law and order and traffic safety.
Public Buildings Expenditures (PBLD)	Construction, equipping, and maintenance of general public buildings not allocated to particular functions.
Public Welfare Expenditures (PWEL)	Support of and assistance to needy persons contingent upon their need.
Sanitation Expenditures (SANT)	Street cleaning, and collection and disposal of garbage and other waste. Sanitary and storm sewers and sewage disposal facilities.
Total Capital Expenditures (TCAP)	Direct expenditure for contract or construction of buildings, roads, and other improvements, and for purchases of equipment, land, and existing structures.

TABLE 3-4 (continued)

Item	Definition
Total Utilities Expenditures (TUTL)	Expenditure for construction or acquisition of utility facilities or equipment, for production and distribution of utility commodities and services (except those furnished to parent city) and for interest on utility debt.
Total Personal Services Expenditures (PSER)	Amounts paid for compensation of city officers and employees.
Total Expenditures (TEXP)	All amounts of money paid out by a government other than for retirement of debt, investment in securities, extension of credit, or as agency transactions. Expenditure includes only external transactions of a government.

examined) are shown for each of the four groups in Table 3-5 (pp. 28-29). A number of observations can be made from the table about the variables and differences across groups.

Generally, the ratios are fairly stable between the 1973 and 1979 periods, indicating the average revenue and expenditure compositions do not change substantially over time. This fact should facilitate planning for and control of the variables. Of those items that did change, outside revenue increased while property tax and own revenue decreased across all groups of the period. Thus, most cities appear to have become more reliant on intergovernmental funds during the time period studies.[10] Expenditures for financial administration, housing and sanitation, total capital expenditures, and total expenditures all increased in proportion to total revenue during the period for all groups. Expenditures for health and hospitals, public welfare and personal services declined in proportion to total revenue for the period.

The magnitude of a few ratios varied in relation to the level of per capita income. Low income cities (Groups 1 and 3) demonstrated greater reliance on outside revenue during the period. In addition, these cities spent a higher proportion of total revenue, on average, for

---

[10]The "taxpayers' revolt," economic recession, and presidential economic policies of the early 1980s all tend to modify these relationships. In general, federal transfers to local governments can be expected to decrease.

health and hospital services. Lower percentages were spent by these cities on highways, parks and recreation, and police services.

A larger number of ratios varied in relation to the level of growth in per capita income experienced by the cities. Low growth cities (Groups 1 and 2) demonstrated higher reliance on property taxes and higher relative expenditures for education, fire, housing and personal services. These cities demonstrated lower relative expenditures for interest and utilities.[11] The classification of cities into homogeneous socio-demographic groups was highly significant for explaining the differences in the ratios for all items except interest, parking, public welfare, and total expenditures. These ratios were not significantly different across groups.

The ability to project budget items across cities in a group depends on the distribution of the ratios within the groups. As we have shown, classifying the cities into homogeneous socio-demographic groups is useful for explaining some of the distributions of ratios across the total sample. The extent to which this classification is useful for projecting budgets of other cities is examined in Chapter 4. The apparent stability of the ratios increases the probability that the averages derived will be useful for predicting and evaluating ratios from other cities.

Another factor that can assist in the prediction process is stability of the ratios across time. If the ratios do not fluctuate to a great extent or if the changes follow a linear growth pattern, predictions of future ratios would be more reliable. Time series models were examined for each ratio for each group.[12] These models indicated that ratios were relatively stable over time. The intercepts of the models generally were significant while the slopes were not. Only about 25% of the variation in ratios for period t could be explained by a growth factor. Thus, changes that do occur in the ratios are not a linear function of time. While this nonsystematic change factor will make prediction more difficult, the small magnitude of the changes over time reduces the risk that the prediction errors will be large.

Average annual growth rates for each ratio for each group are shown in Table 3-6 (p. 30). Almost all of the ratios exhibit small changes during the test period. The largest percentage changes were in small expenditure categories, housing and public welfare.

---

[11] The significance of these differences across groups was assessed by a statistical test of relative differences between and within groups. An Analysis of Variance (ANOVA) test was used for this purpose. The level of significance for each ratio is shown in the last column of Table 3-5.

[12] The models used were first order autoregressive models.

TABLE 3-5
Description of Financial Variables

Variable	Year	Group 1 Mean	Std. Err.	Group 2 Mean	Std. Err.	Group 3 Mean	Std. Err.	Group 4 Mean	Std. Err.	Significance of Group Difference
PTAX	1973	.313	.009	.345	.009	.212	.006	.256	.006	.0001
	1979	.243	.008	.280	.009	.160	.005	.206	.006	.0001
OWNR	1973	.703	.006	.775	.004	.748	.006	.755	.006	.0001
	1979	.658	.006	.761	.005	.717	.006	.739	.005	.0001
OUTR	1973	.297	.006	.225	.004	.255	.006	.245	.006	.0001
	1979	.342	.006	.239	.005	.283	.006	.261	.005	.0001
EDUC	1973	.114	.008	.057	.007	.032	.005	.042	.006	.0001
	1979	.115	.008	.052	.007	.030	.004	.045	.008	.0001
FADM	1973	.016	.001	.019	.001	.016	.001	.017	.001	.0012
	1979	.018	.001	.022	.001	.017	.001	.019	.001	.0023
FIRE	1973	.075	.002	.081	.002	.067	.001	.064	.001	.0001
	1979	.072	.002	.082	.002	.062	.001	.063	.002	.0001
GCONT	1973	.024	.001	.033	.001	.024	.001	.030	.001	.0001
	1979	.027	.001	.036	.001	.023	.001	.031	.001	.0001
HOSP	1973	.035	.004	.016	.002	.033	.004	.014	.003	.0096
	1979	.018	.002	.010	.001	.026	.004	.010	.001	.0104
HIGH	1973	.051	.002	.065	.001	.055	.001	.060	.002	.0002
	1979	.051	.001	.068	.003	.052	.001	.058	.001	.0003

	Year									
HOUS	1973	.013	.001	.009	.001	.007	.001	.006	.001	.0008
	1979	.019	.001	.011	.001	.015	.001	.010	.001	.0009
INTR	1973	.033	.001	.030	.002	.038	.002	.039	.001	.1037
	1979	.029	.001	.031	.002	.035	.002	.038	.001	.1131
PARK	1973	.003	.001	.005	.001	.003	.001	.002	.001	.3862
	1979	.003	.001	.004	.001	.003	.001	.003	.001	.4043
RECR	1973	.031	.001	.046	.001	.033	.001	.044	.001	.0001
	1979	.032	.001	.045	.001	.035	.001	.046	.001	.0001
POLC	1973	.095	.002	.122	.002	.088	.002	.109	.002	.0001
	1979	.095	.002	.134	.004	.085	.002	.113	.002	.0001
PBLD	1973	.010	.001	.012	.001	.007	.001	.010	.001	.0001
	1979	.011	.001	.013	.006	.008	.001	.011	.001	.0004
PWEL	1973	.010	.002	.005	.001	.005	.001	.009	.002	.0971
	1979	.006	.001	.003	.001	.003	.001	.007	.001	.1080
SANT	1973	.053	.002	.064	.002	.068	.002	.067	.002	.0004
	1979	.055	.002	.073	.004	.070	.002	.070	.002	.0006
PSER	1973	.431	.006	.047	.004	.370	.004	.396	.004	.0001
	1979	.404	.005	.423	.007	.348	.004	.381	.003	.0001
TOTL	1973	.130	.008	.104	.005	.199	.009	.137	.006	.0001
	1979	.128	.007	.109	.005	.217	.010	.135	.006	.0001
TCAP	1973	.158	.007	.136	.006	.181	.008	.146	.006	.0001
	1979	.200	.007	.180	.006	.261	.007	.225	.010	.0001
TEXP	1973	.884	.010	.856	.008	.857	.010	.824	.007	.6873
	1979	.956	.006	.970	.015	.972	.008	.952	.007	.7272

TABLE 3-6

Average Annual Growth Rates for Financial Ratios

		Group		
Ratio	1	2	3	4
PTAX	−.032	−.027	−.035	−.028
OWNR	−.009	−.003	−.006	−.003
OUTR	.021	.009	.018	.009
EDUC	.022	−.012	−.009	.010
FADM	.018	.023	.009	.012
FIRE	−.005	.001	−.011	−.001
GCON	.015	.011	−.005	.005
HOSP	−.069	−.049	−.033	−.041
HIGH	−.001	.007	−.007	−.005
HOUS	.066	.017	.163	.077
INTR	−.015	.006	−.011	−.004
PARK	−.003	−.025	−.018	.031
RECR	.002	−.004	.009	.007
POLC	.001	.013	−.004	.005
PBLD	.023	.020	.028	.014
PWEL	−.066	−.004	−.053	−.032
SANT	.022	.020	.004	.006
PSER	−.009	−.005	−.008	−.005
TUTL	−.002	.007	.013	−.002
TCAP	.038	.046	.063	.077
TEXP	.012	.019	.019	.022

Changes in property tax and and total capital expenditures also were relatively large for most groups.

How Good Are the Models?

We have described the tables in this chapter as representing budgeting models when in reality they represent empirical summaries of financial attributes for 780 cities (Table 3-1) or 390 cities (remaining tables). How then are these data useful for budgeting purposes? These steps for preparing a municipal budget are part of the answer to this question.

1. First, determine the socio-demographic classification for the city — in which group does the city fall? Compare socio-demographic attributes for the city to those in Table 3-1, with special reference to per capita income and change in per capita income.
2. Next, select the appropriate formula from Table 3-2 for the identified group. Substitute the city's total revenue (expressed in thousands) for the current year for the symbol TR_{t-1}, perform the mathematical operations, and then budgeted revenue will equal TR_t.
3. Finally, select the appropriate ratios for the group from Table 3-5, and multiply them by budgeted total revenue to derive budget details.

Data in the tables are for fiscal 1979 and must be updated for budgeting more recent periods. The budgeting models demonstrate a method for deriving budgets. Successful implementation of the method would require annual updates of data, as well as modifications to insure that appropriate budget classes are substituted for the ones included in Table 3-5.

Extensive tests were performed to measure the reliability and validity of proposed models, and results of these tests are reported in Appendix B. The remaining 390 cities were used as a "holdout" sample. The models were applied individually to these cities, and variations from expectations were measured. In general, the results of these reliability and validity tests lead us to believe that the models' reliability produces accurate predictions.

Appendix A

Municipal Financial Data

Data contained in the Local Government Financial Data File (LOGOFILE) were obtained from the U.S. Department of Commerce, Bureau of the Census. The Bureau of the Census collects data on local government finances annually and uses these data in preparing reports published by the Bureau. Much of the data included in LOGOFILE appear in *City Government Finances* and *County Government Finances,* published annually.

The Census captures the data in a uniform format and transcribes them to a computer file which contains approximately 400 data items for all municipalities with populations of 25,000 or greater and for a large sample of smaller units. Unfortunately, the Census data are difficult to use in their raw state because of the low level of aggregation and the volume of material which must be processed for individual years. A merged file which contains time series data for a single unit is not available from the Bureau. Accordingly, the cost of utilizing the raw data files is prohibitive.

Other than a population variable, the data collected by the Census consist of certain asset, liability, revenue, and expenditure items as determined by the municipalities' accounting systems. The financial data, however, represent consolidated information about revenue sources, expenditure purposes, and the functions of certain assets and liabilities rather than traditional fund accounting classifications.

Many municipalities do not maintain fixed asset records, so only certain current asset and long-term investment data appear in the file. These include cash, deposits, and security investments. Unfortunately, unrestricted assets are not clearly distinguished from restricted assets. Interfund receivables, however, are omitted.

Similarly, interfund payables are omitted from liabilities, which consist only of short-term and long-term interest bearing obligations. Information on accounts payable, like accounts receivable, is

33

not available. Long-term debt is distinguished by purpose, and information about debt retirement and issuance is available. Pension liability data are not collected, and this information cannot be determined from the accounting records of many municipalities. Fund balance data are not collected and probably would not be meaningful apart from fund classifications.

Thus, the data available do not permit balance sheet construction, either by fund or on a consolidated basis. The asset and liability data are useful primarily for assessment of debt position or the construction of specific financial ratios.

Revenue and expenditure data are much more complete. Revenues are identified by source and function, and expenditures are identified by purpose. Current operating expenditures are separated from capital outlays. These data may be useful for analysis of program operations and for assessment of operating trends. Only actual revenues and expenditures are reported, and, consequently, comparison of data on the file with budgeted amounts is not possible.

LOGOFILE is a transformation of the Census data to a more efficient form for research purposes (see Ingram and Copeland, 1982). Data from the Census files have been aggregated into 111 classes, and null sets have been eliminated to increase the efficiency of the file. LOGOFILE has reorganized the Census variables into a relatively concise set which reflects a traditional accounting report scheme.

The file currently contains eight years (1973 to 1980) of data for all cities and counties included on the Census master file for which all years of data are available. Data on approximately 2,600 entities are included. The file will be updated each year as new data become available. Census data normally are available in October or November of each year for the preceding year (fiscal periods ending in that calendar year).

The data in LOGOFILE have been randomly validated by comparison with Bureau of the Census publications. Accordingly, we believe the data are consistent with the underlying source. The Census data themselves, however, are susceptible to normal errors of omission, transposition, and so on. Little is known of the nature, magnitude, or frequency of errors in the source data but from our experience in using the data we believe these to be slight.

Appendix B

Model Validation

For the revenue and expenditure patterns described to be useful in planning and control purposes, they must be applicable beyond the specific sample or time period used to derive the models. That is, they must be applicable to a broader sample. The time series stability of the ratios was examined for the sample to derive the models in an earlier section. In this section, the application of the models to a holdout sample and the predictive ability of the models for one set of municipalities in one time period, for another set of municipalities in a future time period, are assessed.

Table B-1 provides descriptive statistics for the holdout sample. The average ratios for each financial variable for each sociodemographic class for 1979 are shown. Comparison to Table 3-5 reveals that the means are very similar between the two samples. The mean difference is a measure of the differences between the average values of each ratio for each of the two samples. The mean squared error is a measure of the average difference for each observation (municipality) in the holdout sample from the mean value of the sample used to derive the models. This measure is useful for assessing the statistical significance of the differences between the two samples. Only the values for educational expenditures were significantly different at a probability level of .05 for any of the groups. Educational expenditures were statistically different for each group except Group 3.

The forecasting ability of the models can be observed from Table B-2. The means for each of the ratios for the original sample from 1978 were used to predict the ratios for 1979 for the holdout sample. Mean squared error and mean differences are described. The numbers follow patterns similar to Table B-1. Again, only educational expenditures are significantly different at a probability level of .05.

Both the tests of cross-sectional and time series validity in-

TABLE B-1
Descriptive Statistics for Holdout Sample

Financial Variable	Group 1 Mean	Group 1 Mean Squared Error	Group 1 Mean Difference	Group 2 Mean	Group 2 Mean Squared Error	Group 2 Mean Difference	Group 3 Mean	Group 3 Mean Squared Error	Group 3 Mean Difference	Group 4 Mean	Group 4 Mean Squared Error	Group 4 Mean Difference
PTAX	.016	.016	−.004	.262	.018	−.009	.166	.006	.003	.215	.009	.006
OWNR	.065	.009	.007	.757	.006	−.002	.722	.008	.002	.733	.006	.002
OUTR	.335	.009	−.007	.243	.006	.002	.279	.008	−.002	.267	.006	.002
EDUC	.108	.017	−.007	.056	.012	.002	.032	.002	−.006	.080	.023	.014
FADM	.018	.000	.000	.024	.000	.000	.017	.000	.000	.019	.000	.000
FIRE	.074	.001	.002	.079	.001	−.001	.062	.000	.000	.064	.001	.000
GCON	.027	.000	.000	.038	.000	.000	.022	.000	.000	.031	.000	.000
HOSP	.018	.001	.000	.007	.000	−.001	.022	.002	−.002	.011	.000	.000
HIGH	.051	.000	.000	.070	.003	.000	.052	.000	.000	.058	.000	.000
HOUS	.019	.000	.000	.011	.000	.000	.013	.000	−.001	.010	.000	.000
INTR	.029	.000	.000	.032	.001	.000	.037	.001	.001	.038	.000	.000
PARK	.003	.000	.000	.004	.000	.000	.003	.000	.000	.003	.000	.000
RECR	.032	.000	.000	.048	.000	.002	.034	.000	−.001	.045	.000	.000
POLC	.096	.001	.001	.144	.005	.005	.082	.001	−.001	.112	.001	.000
PBLD	.011	.000	.000	.014	.000	.001	.009	.000	−.001	.010	.000	.000
PWEL	.005	.000	.000	.002	.000	.000	.003	.000	.000	.005	.000	−.001
SANT	.056	.001	−.001	.074	.001	.000	.074	.001	.002	.070	.001	.000
PSER	.407	.006	.003	.433	.020	.005	.335	.005	−.006	.383	.003	.001
TUTL	.130	.014	.002	.107	.006	−.001	.229	.022	−.006	.128	.008	−.003
TCAP	.208	.016	.008	.200	.011	.010	.260	.012	−.001	.203	.029	−.009
TEXP	.959	.014	.003	1.006	.024	.017	.963	.014	−.005	.952	.010	.000

36

TABLE B-2

Statistics for Predictive Validity

Financial Variable	Group 1 Mean Squared Error	Group 1 Mean Difference	Group 2 Mean Squared Error	Group 2 Mean Difference	Group 3 Mean Squared Error	Group 3 Mean Difference	Group 4 Mean Squared Error	Group 4 Mean Difference
PTAX	.016	−.015	.018	−.022	.006	.000	.009	−.002
OWNR	.009	.005	.006	−.004	.008	.006	.006	.001
OUTR	.009	−.005	.006	.004	.008	−.006	.006	−.001
EDUC	.017	−.007	.012	.003	.002	−.007	.023	.015
FADM	.000	.001	.000	.000	.000	.000	.000	.000
FIRE	.001	.001	.001	−.004	.004	−.001	.001	.000
GCON	.000	.000	.000	.000	.000	−.001	.000	.000
HOSP	.001	.001	.000	.000	.002	−.001	.000	.000
HIGH	.000	.000	.003	−.002	.002	.002	.000	.000
HOUS	.000	.002	.000	.000	.001	.000	.000	−.002
INTR	.000	.000	.001	.002	.001	.001	.000	.001
PARK	.000	.000	.000	.000	.000	.001	.000	.000
RECR	.000	.000	.000	.000	.000	−.001	.000	.000
POLC	.001	.000	.005	.003	.000	−.002	.001	.000
PBLD	.000	.001	.000	.000	.000	.000	.000	−.001
PWEL	.000	−.001	.000	−.001	.000	.000	.000	−.001
SANT	.001	.001	.005	.000	.001	.001	.001	.002
PSER	.006	.001	.012	−.027	.005	−.006	.003	.005
TUTL	.014	.004	.006	−.001	.022	.005	.008	−.001
TCAP	.016	−.003	.011	−.004	.012	.001	.029	−.015
TEXP	.014	−.003	.015	−.030	.014	.006	.010	.002

dicate that the models provide reliable measures of the revenue and expenditure policies of municipalities after considering the effects of socio-demographic attributes. Thus, the models should provide useful norms against which the specific activities of individual cities can be measured.

Chapter 4

Budget and Cost Evaluation Procedures

Budgets or plans for future municipal operations frequently rely upon knowledge of past events and established relationships. For each city, the constituents' needs for public goods and services usually are similar from year to year. Furthermore, the municipal resources and systems available for delivering public goods and services are relatively stable from year to year. Given the availability of a particular mix of resources, a plan can be generated to meet constituents' needs. As already shown, most of the stable elements, which relate resources and means for delivering them with constituents' needs, are well described by the socio-demographic group to which a city belongs. Group norms jointly determine the cross-sectional and time series properties of financial relationships underlying the production and distribution of public goods and services. Knowledge of these relationships provides a framework for preparing and evaluating operating budgets.

Of course, each city within a socio-demographic group differs as to resources available and specific constituent needs. Group norms can indicate only broad benchmarks bearing on policy judgments. In and of themselves, group norms rarely can provide absolute standards for evaluating operational performance because they fail to fully reflect unique attributes of individual cities. The same process, however, used to identify group norms can be applied to city-specific data to derive city-specific norms.

Group Policy Budgets

A "group policy" budget can be devised for any city by determining its socio-demographic group. To illustrate this process, assume that Example City belongs to Group 1 (low income, low growth) and that we wish to prepare a group policy budget. Furthermore, assume that total revenue for the prior year amounted to $1,000,000. If the total revenue production function is approximately linear over short periods of time, as shown in Figure 3-1, expected "group policy" revenue for the current year would be approximately $1,132,000 (based on the percentage change in the group revenue index from Table 3-3, e.g., 1.63/1.44 = 1.132; 1.132 × $1,000,000 = $1,132,000). The complete group policy budget could be calculated by multiplying the group cross-sectional relationship factors (percentages) from Table 3-5 times the predicted total revenue, as shown in Table 4-1. For example, the first item, property tax, is found by multiplying .264 (the Group 1 factor in Table 3-5) by $1,132,000, to derive $299,000.

The group policy budget can be used to provide guidance in the preparation of operating plans. The value for each line item reflects the growth and cross-sectional relationship applicable to the group, somewhat similar to the industry-wide standards employed in many industrial situations. Budget requests from individual departments can be compared to the group policy budget to determine the reasonableness of the requests relative to "industry" averages.

City-Specific Budgets

The same techniques described earlier for measuring group norms can be applied to the actual historical operating data for a city to determine specific norms. These would be based upon the unique environment and operating characteristics of the city (this process will parallel, in many cases, the method actually used by the city to prepare the budget). Revenue projections for the current fiscal year would be made by multiplying total revenue for the prior year ($1,000,000) by the specific norm index for revenue growth (assumed in this case to be 1.141). The remaining line items of the specific norm budget would be obtained by multiplying the expected specific norm revenue of $1,141,000 for the current year by the specific cross-sectional production function factors. These would parallel the group factors shown in Table 3-5 but would be based on historical data for the individual city. A specific norm budget, reflecting (hypothetical) city-specific projections, is contained in column 2 of Table 4-2, for the current fiscal year of Example City.

Based on its individual trends (or other estimation methods), the city projects the amounts shown in the specific norm budget column.

TABLE 4-1

Group Policy Budget for a Low Income, Low Growth City

	Projected Total Revenue = $1,132,000	
	Projected Budget Categories	
Category	Amount per Revenue $*	Total Amount (in Thousands)
Revenues		
PTAX	.264	[$299]**
OWNR	.661	748
OUTR	.339	384
Total Revenue	1,000	$1,132
Expenditures		
EDUC	.114	$129
FADM	.017	19
FIRE	.073	83
GCONT	.027	31
HOSP	.017	19
HIGH	.050	57
HOUS	.015	17
INTR	.030	34
PARK	.003	3
RECR	.031	35
POLC	.097	110
PBLD	.010	11
PWEL	.006	7
SANT	.055	62
PSER**	.408	[462]
TOTU	.123	139
TCAP	.221	250
Other***	.078	88
		1,094
Projected Surplus		$ 38

*Averages for Group 1 for prior year.
**Numbers in brackets are subcategories of other numbers in column and were not added separately to the total. For example, PTAX is part of OWNR.
***Difference between total of expenditure categories and TEXP (Total Expenditures)

TABLE 4-2

City Projection Compared to Group Policy Budget
(Numbers in thousands)

Category	Group Policy Budget	Specific Norm Budget	Variance
PTAX	[$299]*	[$320]	[$21]
OWNR	748	762	14
OUTR	384	379	(5)
Total Revenue	1,132	1,141	9
EDUC	129	132	3
FADM	19	22	3
FIRE	83	80	(3)
GCONT	31	33	1
HOSP	19	18	(1)
HIGH	57	56	(1)
HOUS	17	18	1
INTR	34	37	3
PARK	3	5	2
RECR	35	37	2
POC	110	107	(3)
PBLD	11	12	1
PWEL	7	7	0
SANT	62	64	2
PSER	[462]	[474]	[12]
TOTU	139	141	2
TCAP	250	261	11
Other	88	94	6
TEXP	1,094	1,124	30
Projected Surplus	$38	$17	$(21)

*Numbers in brackets were not added separately to column totals.

Management can now evaluate the reasonableness of these projections and can evaluate the reasons for the variances. For example, the city has projected total revenue of $1,141,000, indicating perceived growth in resources beyond the amount that would be typical for Group 1 cities. Property taxes are expected to increase by $21,000 more than is shown in the pro forma budget for Group 1. Perhaps the city expects to revalue taxable property or increase its tax rate, or perhaps the projection is optimistic. Each of the revenue and expenditure categories could be evaluated in the same manner. A problem arises, however, in comparing the two estimates because the revenue bases are not equal. This problem gives rise to another planning technique that can be implemented from the data previously described.

Flexible Budgets

Management is not limited to a pro forma budget based on the historical trend in revenues. It can project budgets at other levels of revenue to identify the potential effect of these changes on operating plans. Flexible budgeting may be particularly useful in this analysis.

Table 4-3 illustrates a comparison between a group policy budget based on Group 1 norms and a projected total revenue of $1,141,000, in agreement with the city's own estimates. The first column of numbers is calculated by multiplying the factors from Table 3-5 times projected revenue of $1,141,000. The second column is the same as column 2 in Table 4-2. The third column is the difference between columns 1 and 2. Comparisons now can be made on a common basis. Projected property taxes are still considerably higher than the norm, and management should satisfy itself that the projection is reasonable.

Differences in expenditure categories also can be examined. Attention might focus on why less than average expenditures are being made for police and fire protection and why salary (PSER) and capital expenditures are higher than average. These differences may be explained by population characteristics, by age of the city's infrastructure, and so on, or the difference may be due to inefficiency or poor planning within certain departments.

Control of Operations

Once actual results have been determined, the group norms can be useful for evaluating actual operating results from a control perspective and can help identify the causes of unexpected events.

A preliminary analysis of actual results can be made by adding an additional column of operating results to Table 4-3 and by examining resulting variances. Assume that actual results for Example City were as shown in column 3 of Table 4-4. The city's operating results are compared to group norms that were projected at the beginning

TABLE 4-3

Comparison of City Projection to Flexible Group Norm Budget
(Numbers in thousands)

Category	Flexible Budget	Specific Norm Budget	Variance
PTAX	[$301]*	[$320]	[$19]
OWNR	754	762	12
OUTR	387	379	(12)
Total Revenue	1,141	1,141	0
EDUC	130	132	2
FADM	19	22	3
FIRE	83	80	(3)
GCONT	31	33	2
HOSP	19	18	(1)
HIGH	57	56	(1)
HOUS	17	18	1
INTR	34	37	3
PARK	3	5	2
RECR	35	37	2
POC	111	107	(4)
PBLD	11	12	1
PWEL	7	7	0
SANT	63	64	1
PSER	[466]	[474]	[8]
TOTU	140	141	1
TCAP	252	261	9
Other	89	94	5
TEXP	1,102	1,124	22
Projected Surplus	$39	$17	$(22)

*Numbers in brackets were not added separately to column totals.

of the year and to the city's own specific norms. These differences may help isolate reasons for the results in various categories and may be useful for planning for future operations.

For example, in this illustration, the city overestimated revenues and expenditures while the group norms underestimated these amounts. The city might consider revising its budgeting procedures to incorporate some weighting of the group norms. The variances in Table 4-4 are similar to market variances in corporate cost account-

TABLE 4-4

Comparison of Actual with Projected Results
(Numbers in thousands)

Category	(1) Group Norm (from Table 4-1)	(2) External Variance (3-1)	(3) Actual	(4) Internal Variance (3-5)	(5) Specific Norm (from Table 4-2)
PTAX	[$299]*	$13	[$312]	($8)	[$320]
OWNR	748	11	759	(3)	762
OUTR	384	(8)	376	(3)	379
Total Revenue	1,132	3	1,135	(6)	1,141
EDUC	129	(1)	130	2	132
FADM	19	(1)	10	2	22
FIRE	83	2	81	(1)	80
GCONT	31	(1)	32	1	33
HOSP	19	(1)	20	(2)	18
HIGH	57	(2)	59	(3)	56
HOUS	17	1	16	2	18
INTR	34	(3)	37	0	37
PARK	3	(1)	4	1	5
RECR	35	(2)	37	0	37
POLC	110	1	109	(2)	107
PBLD	11	(1)	12	0	12
PWEL	7	0	7	0	7
SANT	62	1	61	3	64
PSER	[462]	(11)	[473]	1	[474]
TOTU	139	(1)	140	1	141
TCAP	250	(5)	255	6	261
Other	88	(7)	95	(1)	94
TEXP	1,094	(21)	1,115	9	1,124
Projected Surplus	$38	($18)	$20	$3	$17

*Numbers in brackets were not added separately to column totals.

ing in that they indicate the magnitude of unexpected results because of the failure of the city to operate at a predetermined level of services. Thus, the hypothetical city-generated revenues that were $3,000 in excess of the group norm but $6,000 less than it anticipated. It incurred expenditures that were $21,000 more than the group norm but were $9,000 less than it anticipated.

An even more useful analysis would compare actual results to flexible budgets prepared from both group and city data. This analysis would describe what the results should have been at the actual level of revenues. The total variances produced by these comparisons would be useful for estimating how well the city performed compared to other cities, given projections available at the beginning of the year. This analysis will be presented for actual city data in Chapter 5.

In addition, management could evaluate how well the city performed in comparison to other cities' actual results. Table 4-5 describes group norms based on current year actual results. Total revenues for Group 1 cities increased at an actual average rate of 9.2%. Example City should have generated revenues of $1,092,000 ($1,000,000 × 1.092). The first column in Table 4-5 was calculated by multiplying the Group 1 factors in Table 3-5 times $1,092,000. Column 5 numbers were calculated by multiplying the Group 1 factors in Table 3-5 times actual revenue of $1,135,000.

The second column (variances) reveals that the city generated $43,000 of revenues in excess of the average for a Group 1 city with prior year operating revenues of $1,000,000. The city also incurred expenses that were $71,000 higher than the average for Group 1 and $30,000 higher than the average for Group 1 cities which generated $1,135,000 in total revenues. Management can determine whether these results are reasonable and in line with its own operating goals.

Departmental Application

The analysis based on the data in Chapter 3 provides only general guidance as to the causes of differences from planned operations and provides only general guidelines for determining remedial actions. More detailed analysis is possible using similar techniques to those above if specific data are available for each department, program or function. Total variances can be separated into price and efficiency variances permitting more detailed performance evaluation.

In the following example, more information about specific departmental operations is assumed than for the general models examined

TABLE 4-5

Comparison of Group and City Results
(Numbers in thousands)

Category	(1) Group Norm at Expected Revenue	(2) Variance (3-1)	(3) Actual	(4) Variance (3-5)	(5) Group Norm at Actual Revenue
PTAX	[$265]*	[$47]	[$312]	[$36]	[$276]
OWNR	719	40	759	12	747
OUTR	373	3	376	(12)	388
Total Revenue	1,092	43	1,135	0	1,135
EDUC	126	(4)	130	1	131
FADM	20	0	20	0	20
FIRE	79	(2)	81	1	82
GCONT	29	(3)	32	(1)	31
HOSP	20	0	20	0	20
HIGH	57	(2)	59	(1)	58
HOUS	21	5	16	6	22
INTR	32	(5)	37	(4)	33
PARK	3	(1)	4	(1)	3
RECR	35	(2)	37	(1)	36
POLC	104	(5)	109	(1)	108
PBLD	12	0	12	0	12
PWEL	7	0	7	0	7
SANT	60	(1)	61	1	62
PSER	[437]	[36]	[473]	[14]	[459]
TOTU	140	0	140	5	145
TCAP	218	(37)	255	28	227
TEXP	$1,044	[$71]	$1,115	($30)	$1,085

*Numbers in brackets were not added separately to column totals.

in the prior discussion. For example, costs that vary in relationship to the level of operations (variable costs) are separated from costs that do not vary with the level of operations (fixed costs).

In a commercial enterprise, revenues also are a function of operating level. Frequently, this relationship does not hold for municipal services. Instead, revenues are budgeted to match expected total expenditures or vice versa. This budgeting process

47

leads to the relationship between revenues and expenditures, described in the previous section, in which expenditures can be observed to vary in relationship to revenues without consideration of fixed and variable components. Thus, the prior discussion did not assume that all costs are variable. It only demonstrated that incremental budgeting produces a predictable link between changes in revenue and changes in expenditure.

For control purposes, a detailed analysis of departmental efficiency can be obtained by considering costs in relation to the level of operating activity in addition to the analysis of expenditures and revenues described above. This analysis provides more depth than was possible with the more general models assumed before.

For purposes of illustration, a municipal fire department has been selected as a specific type of municipal entity to which standard costing and flexible budgeting can be applied.[1] A fire department has several functional objectives that can be isolated for further analysis. The same process can be readily applied to individual station activities, other department programs, or to almost any municipal activity. Fire protection may be one of the more difficult areas for application of these managerial techniques because little influence can be exerted over the level of activity necessary to control fires. Resources, however, are applied to the fire control division in anticipation of a forecast level and intensity of fires. Our purpose here is to provide some guidance for evaluating the performance of this division as well as the level of resources devoted to this program.

The flexible budgeting technique can be used for managerial purposes to analyze the economic impact of activity variations, price changes, and performance attainments. In this manner, insight into program efficiency and effectiveness can be achieved. Table 4-6 provides a typical program cost and budget comparison for a small fire department. Actual expenditures for four typical programs are compared to the program budgets and variances are separated. This information provides considerably more information than the conventional line item record of expenditures. These data, however, are only a summary and provide a starting point for further analysis.

The first step in the analysis is represented by the approved legal budget. For further analysis it is necessary to isolate the activity level and related costs per unit represented by this budget, and a common activity base must be derived for this purpose. In many cases more than one denominator may be necessary, depending on

---

[1] For further discussion see Holder and Ingram [1976].

TABLE 4-6
Program Costs and Budget Comparisons

	Fire Control	Fire Prevention	Training	Administration	Total	Budget	Variance
Personnel Services	$45,000	$2,000	$1,000	$10,000	$58,000	$56,000	($2,000)
Supplies & Other	5,000	2,000	1,000	1,000	9,000	10,000	1,000
Maintenance	2,000	1,000	1,000	0	4,000	5,000	1,000
Utilities	2,000	0	0	1,000	3,000	4,000	1,000
Capital Outlay	7,000	0	0	0	7,000	5,000	(2,000)
Total	$61,000	$5,000	$3,000	$12,000	$81,000	$80,000	($1,000)

types of activities. For the fire control program, work hours have been selected as the denominator most applicable.

Table 4-7 provides data on the average amount of time spent in fire control activities based on historical records. The expected quantity of fires also is developed from historical data. From this information, the total expected work hours can be computed. Data are provided for the fire control program only, and a single-station department is assumed. Again, similar procedures can be used for other programs and for multiple-station departments.

In order to perform the most realistic and meaningful cost analysis from a managerial point of view, actual performance should be compared with a budget based upon the actual level of activity achieved instead of the forecast level of activity. Such a budget is illustrated in Table 4-8. The procedures necessary for the successful construction of the management flexible budget for the actual activity level achieved are:

1. determination of normal activity level (work hours),
2. estimation of per unit costs at this level of activity (budget), and
3. application of these standards to the activity level achieved (flexible budget).

For example, it is estimated that fires requiring 1,755 work hours will occur during the coming year (computed in Table 4-7). At this activity and mix level, it further is estimated that $59,000 (the budget amount) will be required to adequately control anticipated fires.

TABLE 4-7

Determination of Activity Level

Fire Type	Expected Quantity	Average Time (Work Hours)	Annual Forecast (Work Hours)
Residential	45	15	675
Commercial	28	20	560
Industrial	16	25	400
Other	12	10	120
Total work hours forecast			1,175

This information allows the preparer to develop appropriate cost rates per work hour which can then be applied to the actual activity level achieved (see Table 4-8). Total expected work hours are determined based upon the actual number of fires experienced. Costs are then forecast based upon the level of activity achieved. Variable costs are expected to change depending upon activity levels and are therefore anticipated. Fixed costs, however, remain constant as activity varies.

The final step in this analysis requires the division of the gross variances isolated in Table 4-8 into underlying causal components.

TABLE 4-8

Comparison of Budget with Cost at Actual Level of Activity

	Budget	Flexible Budget	Actual	Variance
Fires:				
Residential	45	49	49	
Commercial	28	26	26	
Industrial	16	12	12	
Other	12	18	18	
Total Incidents	101	105	105	
Work Hours	1,755	1,735	1,810	75
Variable Costs:				
Salaries	$25,000	$24,714*	$30,000	$5,284
Supplies & other	6,000	5,932	5,000	(932)
Maintenance	5,000	4,943	2,000	(2,943)
Utilities	3,000	2,966	2,000	(966)
Total Variable Cost	$39,000	$38,555	$39,000	$ 445
Fixed Costs:				
Supervision & salaries	$15,000	$15,000	$15,000	0
Capital	5,000	5,000	7,000	$2,000
Total Costs	$59,000	$58,555	$61,000	$2,445

*Numbers are calculated by dividing budget by expected work hours and multiplying times flexible budget work hours. For example, $24,714 = ($25,000/1,755) × 1,735.

51

The initial effect displayed in Table 4-9 will divide the total $2,444 variance into subparts. The price variance compares the actual costs incurred with the total costs expected at the activity level achieved, fixed costs being included at the amount anticipated. Variable costs are extended by the variable cost rate to reflect total variable costs expected at the actual level of activity. Also, the price variance displays the economic impact of deviations in actual spending levels from those planned as a result of price changes encountered during the period. The effects of activity level fluctuations are removed from this analysis.

The efficiency variance isolated relates to the cumulative amount of time required to control the actual fires encountered. Because each type of fire considered has been assigned an average time based upon historical performance, this variance is useful in quantifying the economic impact of a shift in mix or severity of fires controlled. It took 1,810 work hours to control fires that historically should have taken 1,735 work hours. One cannot conclude, however, that this is unfavorable, per se. This statistic indicates that the fires may have been more severe or complicated than expected and thus may have required additional resources to control. Nevertheless, the early detection of such trends and related economic consequences provides relevant information for future planning and budgeting.

Although the total variance has been divided into underlying components, additional analysis may still be desirable to identify line item cost variances. Each line item expense in the fire control division can be analyzed in the same manner as the previous discussion. The identification of additional specific variance components may sometimes be desired. This is especially true of items which may possess controllable and uncontrollable characteristics. An example of this situation might arise from the desire to identify the impact of inflation on departmental costs.

In the last example, the spending variance was unfavorable. The full significance of this fact is not apparent, however, until it is recognized that prices may have increased during the year at a rate faster than originally anticipated.

Standard costing and flexible budgeting are logical complements to an operating budgeting system. The determination of program objectives requires in many cases the projection of specific costs which are made possible by standard costing. For example, setting a quota for the number of fire prevention lectures or training activities to be held in a particular period of time requires forecasting the costs of these activities. The benefits actually achieved must be compared to the predetermined objectives and to the costs involved.

TABLE 4-9

Fire Control Total Cost Variance Analysis

Actual Cost	Budget Cost × Actual Time	Budget Cost × Budget Time
	Fixed Cost = $20,000	Fixed Cost = $20,000
	Variable Cost	Variable Cost = $38,556
	($22.22* × 1,810) = 40,218	
$61,000	Total = $60,218	Total = $58,556
	Price Variance = $782 U Efficiency Variance = $1,662 U	
	Total Variance $2,444 U	

*Budget rate = Budget Cost/Budget Time = $38,556/1,735 = $22.22

Standard costing is consequently a tool for evaluating the objectives and benefits to be derived. In order to assess properly the value of the achieved results, actual costs should be compared to projections according to actual activity levels, necessitating the use of flexible budgets. Efficiency is relative depending on the level of operating activity. Accordingly, the evaluation of efficiency should make use of a flexible standard which can then be related to the actual activity experienced.

Standards such as those used in a standard costing system uncover certain types of inefficiencies regarding the purchase or use of resources and allow for some additional comparison between operating units, such as fire stations. This information can be used by the public to determine where resources are being allocated most efficiently and is especially useful for internal management for personnel evaluation and resource allocation.

Standard costing and flexible budgeting require relatively little additional data collection or manipulation. Detailed cost records are required for program budgeting, and actual activity levels are easily determinable from operating reports. Standards can be determined from historical data and current price lists. The process of computing standards, flexible budgets, and variances requires time but can be computerized for use by larger municipalities.

Chapter 5

Descriptive Analysis for Specific Cases

The planning and control techniques which have been considered for one hypothetical city can be extended by applying the proposed evaluation technique to actual data for several cities. The socio-demographic attributes of the six cities chosen differed widely from each other because the cities were selected to demonstrate the applicability of our technique to cities facing different underlying circumstances. Financial data for each of the cities were evaluated relative to that of cities in similar socio-demographic circumstances such as described in Chapter 3.

Four comparisons are made for each case and each comparison describes a slightly different approach to evaluating a given city's fiscal performance relative to its group norms. Given the underlying differences among the six cities, the analyses encompass a broad range of situations that are likely to be encountered in typical studies. These illustrations are intended only to demonstrate the application of the evaluation techniques previously described. More specific analysis would be possible, given detailed operating records typically available to municipal management.

Four sets of budgets are prepared for each of the six cities. The first set consists of prospective budgets based upon prior year actual revenue for the city, adjusted to reflect expected group norm revenue growth estimated from prior year data. The second set also is prospective in that it also starts with prior year actual revenue for the city, but these numbers are adjusted to reflect city-specific revenue growth estimated from city historical data. The third and fourth sets of budgets are retrospective and start with current year actual revenues for each city.

Values for each line item within each budget are determined by multiplying estimated total revenue by a pre-established set of factors representing the cross-sectional relationship between all of the items within the budget. The first set of budgets is based upon the prior year cross-sectional relationship found within the sociodemographic group to which the city belongs, and the resulting budget is called a group norm prospective budget. The second set of budgets is based on the cross-sectional relationship which describes the city's fiscal structure as of the prior year, and these are called city-specific prospective budgets. The third set of budgets is similar to the first set, except the cross-sectional relationships are specified retrospectively based upon current year group norm relationships. The fourth set is based upon retrospective city-specific fiscal relationships for the current year; that is, they reflect current year actual fiscal data.

Variances can be calculated between each set of budgets by subtracting one of the pair of values for each line item from the other value. These variances can support evaluations that provide insight into managerial performance of municipal operations similar to that available in industrial situations in an analysis of variance from standard costs. This theme will be developed in more detail with reference to the specific cases described below.

Case A: Basic Analysis

Case A concerns a city that has experienced high income and low growth similar to other cities found in Socio-Demographic Group 2. Table 5-1 provides a comparison of actual revenues and expenses for the current year, relative to a city-specific budget and to a group norm budget. The first column of numbers represents the group norm budget. These projections were based on the actual prior year total revenue for Case A, the actual prior year average growth rate for Group 2 (high income, low growth cities) and the cross-sectional relationship between revenues and expenditures for Group 2 cities for the prior year. For example, the actual total revenue for Case A in the prior year was $12,778,000, and the average growth rate for Group 2 was approximately 16%, thus, the group norm budget shows TREV of $14,822,000 for the current year ($12,778,000 × 1.16). The prior year PTAX/TREV factor for Group 2 was .308. Accordingly the group norm budget shows PTAX for the current year of $4,565,000 ($14,822,000 × .308).

The group norm budget indicates how much revenue the city should have expected in the current year, assuming that its year-to-year revenue growth was equal to the growth rate for other cities in

TABLE 5-1

Case A — Budget Evaluation
(Numbers in thousands)

Ratio	Prior Year Group Norm Budget	Policy Variances	Actual Results	Performance Variances	Prior Year Flexible Budget
PTAX	4.565	−1.140	3.425	−0.642	4.067
OWNR	11.354	−2.059	9.295	−0.821	10.116
OUTR	3.468	0.443	3.911	0.821	3.090
TREV	14.822	−1.616	13.206	0.000	13.206
EDUC	1.467	1.418	0.049	1.258	1.307
FADM	0.356	−0.063	0.293	0.024	0.317
FIRE	1.290	−0.581	0.709	0.440	1.149
GCON	0.548	−0.200	0.348	0.141	0.489
HOSP	0.178	−0.107	0.071	0.087	0.158
HIGH	1.023	0.000	1.023	−0.12	0.911
HOUS	0.104	−0.016	0.120	−0.028	0.092
INTR	0.489	−0.567	1.056	−0.620	0.436
PARK	0.059	0.059	0.000	0.053	0.053
RECR	0.711	0.238	0.473	0.161	0.634
POLC	2.046	0.461	1.585	0.237	1.822
PBLD	0.208	0.128	0.080	0.105	0.185
PWEL	0.074	0.074	0.000	0.066	0.066
SANT	1.112	−0.677	1.789	−0.799	0.990
PSER	7.278	3.463	3.815	2.669	6.484
TUTL	1.630	0.770	0.860	0.593	1.453
TCAP	3.113	−1.118	4.231	−1.458	2.773
TEXP	15.875	2.609	13.266	0.878	14.144

Group 2. The group norm budgeted expenditures for Case A presumes that city officials will use revenues to acquire goods and services in a pattern similar to the average relationship found in other Group 2 cities. This expenditure pattern for the current year assumes that city management made financial decisions consistent with the consensus decisions made by managers of similar cities. Parking and welfare services are not provided by this city, as is common for Group 2 cities.

The third column of Table 5-1 describes the actual revenue and expenditure balances for Case A for the current year. These balances are identical to those that would have been produced by city managers who had perfect foresight. The variances in column 2 represent the differences between balances in columns 1 and 3, and these can be interpreted as indicating the consequences of policy choices made by city managers relative to the average policy choice outcomes made by managers of other Group 2 cities.

As a policy choice, management levied a lighter tax burden on its citizens, but sought more revenue from external sources. As a result, total revenue was almost 11% less than would result under Group 2 growth. Lower than average expenditures were anticipated for all services except housing, interest, sanitation, and capital expenditures. Interest expenditures were considerably above the expected norm, reflecting the costs of debt financing for some of the capital expenditures. Highway expenditures were equal to the expected norm, while total expenditures, like total revenue, were below the expected norm. Personal service expenditures were considerably less than the average for the Group 2 cities.

This analysis highlights characteristics of the policy choices for Case A in the current year that distinguish it from the choices made by cities in similar socio-demographic circumstances. In part, these variances may reflect natural differences in physical resources or social differences in citizens' tastes, but most of the variances result from conscious policy choices concerned with the incidence of social costs and the allocation of public resources. Such policy choices may indicate changes in revenue sources or economic shifts that will impact on the ability to acquire resources, or it could be explained by differences in other characteristics of the city such as population age or health.

The variances in column 2 are useful for evaluating actual policy choices but are not particularly useful for evaluating actual performance because they are based on the expected revenue for the city. The last column in Table 5-1 demonstrates the flexible budget for Case A at a revenue level of $13.2 million. The same factors were used in this column as in column one (e.g., PTAX = $4,067,000 = 13,206,000 × .308). The flexible budget indicates the amounts that would have resulted if Group 2 average results had occurred at the level of total revenue actually achieved. The variances in column 4 describe the differences between the city's actual performance and its expected peformance given data during the current year. These numbers are useful for evaluating how the city's performance deviated from expected group norms.

Variances in column 4 generally are smaller than those in column 2. Property taxes and own revenue were still smaller than group averages. Total expenditures were less than average for the actual level of revenues for Group 2 cities. Interest expenditures, capital expenditures, and sanitation expenditures were considerably less. This information should be useful for management decisions during the operating period. Comparisons can be made to the original budget and to the flexible budget norms to determine whether the city is meeting its goals and whether the differences from expectation are reasonable and explainable.

A different form of analysis can be performed after the end of the fiscal year, when actual activity levels for the budget year are known. Table 5-2 provides retrospective comparisons of budget and actual fiscal balances for Case A. The budget is based upon current year Group 2 results. That is, column 1 of Table 5-2 is calculated by multiplying TREV of $13,468,000 times the Group 2 factors for the current year (Table 3-5). Thus, PTAX = $3,771,000 = 13,468,000 × .280. TREV was computed based on the actual Group 2 growth rate of 5.4%, accordingly, $13,468,000 = $12,778,000 (prior year actual TREV × 1.504). The comparisons made in Table 5-2 measure the retrospective performance of Case A relative to the actual performance of similar cities. The first column of Table 5-2 projects the operating performance based on the average revenue growth rate for Group 2 cities for the current year and Group 2 cross-sectional factors. The variances in column 2 reflect the differences between the actual fiscal performance of Case A and Group 2 norms based upon a prior year revenue equal to that of Case A. If the city had responded to the forces underlying average Group 2 economic changes, column 2 variances would all be zero. Nonzero variances could reflect economic or environmental changes that occurred during the current fiscal year.

The variances in column 2 of Table 5-2 are smaller in the current year than in column 2 of Table 5-1. Total revenue was only slightly smaller than expected. Interest, sanitation and capital expenditures were still much higher than the norm. In contrast to Table 5-1, total expenditures are now only slightly higher than average. The personal service expenditure variance is not as large as reflected in Table 5-1.

A final comparison in column 4 is made by computing the variances between actual results and Group 2, current year norms for a revenue level of $13.2 million, an amount equal to the actual revenue realized by Case A. These variances are similar to those in column 2; however, they provide a few additional insights. For example, financial administration expenditures are seen to have been slightly higher than the norm. Total expenditures were even larger than the group norm as were interest, sanitation, and capital expenditures.

TABLE 5-2

Case A — Performance Evaluation
(Numbers in thousands)

Ratio	Current Year Group Norm Budget	Policy Variances	Actual Results	Performance Variances	Current Year Flexible Budget
PTAX	3.771	− 0.346	3.425	− 0.273	3.698
OWNR	10.249	− 0.954	9.295	− 0.755	10.050
OUTR	3.219	0.692	3.911	0.755	3.156
TREV	13.468	− 0.262	13.206	0.000	13.206
EDUC	0.700	0.651	0.049	0.638	0.687
FADM	0.296	0.003	0.293	− 0.002	0.291
FIRE	1.104	0.395	0.709	0.374	1.083
GCON	0.485	0.137	0.348	0.127	0.475
HOSP	0.135	0.064	0.071	0.061	0.132
HIGH	0.916	− 0.107	1.023	− 0.125	0.898
HOUS	0.148	0.028	0.120	0.025	0.145
INTR	0.418	− 0.638	1.056	− 0.647	0.409
PARK	0.054	0.054	0.000	0.053	0.053
RECR	0.606	0.133	0.473	0.121	0.594
POLC	1.805	0.220	1.585	0.185	1.770
PBLD	0.175	0.095	0.080	0.092	0.172
PWEL	0.040	0.040	0.000	0.040	0.040
SANT	0.983	− 0.806	1.789	− 0.825	0.964
PSER	5.697	1.882	3.815	1.771	5.586
TUTL	1.468	0.608	0.860	0.579	1.439
TCAP	2.424	− 1.807	4.231	− 1.854	2.377
TEXP	13.064	− 0.202	13.266	− 0.456	12.810

The comparisons from Table 5-2 may be used for control purposes. Deviations from group norm expectations may reflect inefficiencies in the production and distribution of public goods and services relative to the productive efficiency of similar cities. Steps can be taken to alter operations for functions in which deviations cannot be justified. Future expectations may be altered by these comparisons if they reflect changes in economic attributes or population needs. Evaluations of future fiscal operations should consider the insights learned from current period comparisons.

TABLE 5-3

Case B — Budget Evaluation
(Numbers in thousands)

Ratio	Prior Year Group Norm Budget	Policy Variances	Actual Results	Performance Variances	Prior Year Flexible Budget
PTAX	2.327	0.395	2.722	0.677	2.045
OWNR	9.879	−3.518	6.361	−2.320	8.681
OUTR	4.055	1.828	5.883	2.320	3.563
TREV	13.934	−1.690	12.244	0.000	12.244
EDUC	0.432	0.432	0.000	0.380	0.380
FADM	0.251	0.171	0.080	0.140	0.220
FIRE	0.878	0.274	0.604	0.167	0.771
GCON	0.334	0.142	0.192	0.102	0.294
HOSP	0.251	0.060	0.191	0.029	0.220
HIGH	0.725	−0.444	1.169	−0.532	0.637
HOUS	0.153	−0.327	0.480	−0.345	0.135
INTR	0.488	0.193	0.295	0.134	0.429
PARK	0.042	−0.104	0.146	−0.109	0.037
RECR	0.502	0.038	0.464	−0.023	0.441
POLC	1.212	0.692	0.520	0.545	1.065
PBLD	0.125	−0.030	0.155	−0.045	0.110
PWEL	0.042	0.042	0.000	0.037	0.037
SANT	0.989	0.444	0.545	0.324	0.869
PSER	4.849	0.782	4.067	0.194	4.261
TUTL	3.038	1.490	1.548	1.121	2.669
TCAP	3.595	0.223	3.372	−0.213	3.159
TEXP	13.252	1.797	11.455	0.189	11.644

Case B: Extensions

Case B concerns a Group 3, low income, high growth city. Column 1 of Table 5-3 again shows the projected group norm budget from the previous year's data (calculated in the same manner as Table 5-1). Projected total revenue was $13.9 million, considerably higher than actual revenue of $12.1 million. Own revenue was considerably lower than would have been expected for a Group 3 city if previous group trends had held. Property taxes and outside revenue were higher than expected. Management might examine the reasons for the low magnitude of own revenue, given that property taxes exceed the norms. Other revenue sources might be available that would be more equitable and/or efficient than property taxes.

Some of the expenditure variances indicate that the city did not provide certain services that were normally provided by Group 3 cities. In this example, education and welfare services were not expenditures of the city. Differences in service responsibilities may be observed from this analysis and should be taken into consideration when evaluating the budget and municipal performance.

The variances in column 4 of Table 5-3 indicate differences between actual and projected results at the level of revenues actually achieved. The revenue mix patterns described by the column 2 variances can still be observed. The city's expenditures differed from the average expectation for Group 3 cities in several respects: highway, housing and capital expenditures were higher than projected; police, sanitation and utility expenditures were lower; total expenditures were slightly less than the Group 3 norms; and personal service expenditures differed only slightly from the projected amounts.

Table 5-4 provides comparisons between actual and projected results, wherein the projection reflects actual Group 3, current year norms (calculated in the same manner as Table 5-2). Because the current growth rate for Group 3 cities greatly exceeded that of Case B, a group norm budget based on the city's prior year revenue was considerably higher than the actual revenue level achieved by the city in the current year. The revenue mix pattern of Table 5-3, however, is still revealing. Both variance columns in Table 5-4 provide similar information. The city's expenditures were less than average for most services. Highways and housing expenditures were well above the average of Group 3 cities during the period, and police, sanitation and utility expenditures were considerably lower than average.

Analysis of Specific Factors

Tables 5-5 and 5-6 provide comparative data for two Group 1 (low income, low growth) cities with very different financial patterns. Case C demonstrates a combination of much lower than normal property taxes and higher than normal total revenue. In contrast, Case D demonstrates a pattern consisting of higher than normal property taxes combined with lower than normal own revenue and total revenue. Outside revenue is below normal in Case C but above average in Case D.

TABLE 5-4

Case B — Performance Evaluation
(Numbers in thousands)

Ratio	Current Year Group Norm Budget	Policy Variances	Actual Results	Performance Variances	Current Year Flexible Budget
PTAX	2.194	0.528	2.722	0.763	1.959
OWNR	9.834	−3.473	6.361	−2.418	8.779
OUTR	3.881	2.002	5.883	2.418	3.465
TREV	13.715	−1.471	12.244	0.000	12.244
EDUC	0.411	0.411	0.000	0.367	0.367
FADM	0.233	0.153	0.080	0.128	0.208
FIRE	0.850	0.246	0.604	0.155	0.759
GCON	0.315	0.123	0.192	0.090	0.282
HOSP	0.357	0.166	0.191	0.127	0.318
HIGH	0.713	−0.456	1.169	0.532	0.637
HOUS	0.206	−0.274	0.480	−0.296	0.184
INTR	0.480	0.185	0.295	0.134	0.429
PARK	0.041	−0.105	0.146	−0.109	0.037
RECR	0.480	0.016	0.464	−0.035	0.429
POLC	1.166	0.646	0.520	0.521	1.041
PBLD	0.110	−0.045	0.155	−0.057	0.098
PWEL	0.041	0.041	0.000	0.037	0.037
SANT	0.960	0.415	0.545	0.312	0.857
PSER	4.773	0.706	4.067	0.194	4.261
TUTL	2.976	1.428	1.548	1.109	2.657
TCAP	3.580	0.208	3.372	−0.176	3.196
TEXP	13.331	1.876	11.455	0.446	11.901

Table 5-5 reveals that Case C had actual revenues of $3.7 million more than would have been projected for the average Group 1 city with prior year revenue of $46,660,000. The city's property taxes were $10.8 million less than projected on the basis of revenue production functions similar to the group norm. At the same time, actual total expenditures were less than projected, although some expenditure items such as interest were higher than average.

Appendix A (Performance Evaluation for Case C) indicates that current actual revenues were higher than expected on group norms by a larger amount than expected based on pro forma estimates. Thus, the city's total revenues increased by larger amounts and

TABLE 5-5

Case C — Budget Evaluation
(Numbers in thousands)

Ratio	Prior Year Group Norm Budget	Policy Variances	Actual Results	Performance Variances	Prior Year Flexible Budget
PTAX	13.944	− 9.790	4.154	− 10.760	14.914
OWNR	34.913	5.884	40.797	3.454	37.343
OUTR	17.906	− 2.209	15.697	− 3.454	19.151
TREV	52.819	3.675	56.494	0.000	56.494
EDUC	6.021	6.021	0.000	6.440	6.440
FADM	0.898	0.081	0.817	0.143	0.960
FIRE	3.856	− 1.158	5.014	− 0.890	4.124
GCON	1.426	0.059	1.367	0.158	1.525
HOSP	0.898	0.710	0.188	0.772	0.960
HIGH	2.641	− 0.633	3.274	− 0.449	2.825
HOUS	0.792	− 0.409	1.201	− 0.354	0.847
INTR	1.585	− 5.816	7.401	− 5.706	1.695
PARK	0.158	− 0.029	0.187	− 0.018	0.169
RECR	1.637	− 0.448	2.085	− 0.334	1.751
POLC	5.123	− 1.993	7.116	− 1.636	5.480
PBLD	0.528	− 1.048	1.576	− 1.011	0.565
PWEL	0.317	0.317	0.000	0.339	0.339
SANT	2.905	0.757	2.148	0.959	3.107
PSER	21.550	− 0.285	21.835	1.215	23.050
TUTL	6.497	6.497	0.000	6.949	6.949
TCAP	11.673	− 2.742	14.415	− 1.930	12.485
TEXP	51.023	0.653	50.370	− 4.203	54.573

more rapidly than the growth trends implicit in the group norms. Outside revenue and total expenditures were considerably smaller than the norms.

This example highlights a situation in which a city has responded to constraints on its ability to raise property taxes by utilizing other sources of revenue. It has maintained fiscal viability by restraining expenditures, even though it appears to have a debt burden that exceeds the norm.

In contrast, Case D demonstrates the consequences of revenue patterns that are lower than expected. Table 5-6 indicates that actual revenues were considerably smaller than estimated based on

TABLE 5-6

Case D — Budget Evaluation
(Numbers in thousands)

Ratio	Prior Year Group Norm Budget	Policy Variances	Actual Results	Performance Variances	Prior Year Flexible Budget
PTAX	10.677	− 0.594	10.083	1.647	8.436
OWNR	26.732	− 11.869	14.853	− 6.258	21.121
OUTR	13.710	3.380	17.090	6.258	10.832
TREV	40.442	− 8.489	31.953	0.000	31.953
EDUC	4.610	− 3.234	7.844	− 4.201	3.643
FADM	0.688	0.025	0.663	− 0.120	0.543
FIRE	2.952	1.482	1.470	0.863	2.333
GCON	1.092	0.172	0.920	− 0.057	0.863
HOSP	0.688	0.090	0.598	− 0.055	0.543
HIGH	2.022	1.111	0.911	0.687	1.598
HOUS	0.607	0.146	0.461	0.018	0.479
INTR	1.213	0.544	0.669	0.290	0.959
PARK	0.121	− 0.051	0.172	− 0.076	0.096
RECR	1.254	− 0.254	1.508	− 0.517	0.991
POLC	3.923	2.007	1.916	1.183	3.099
PBLD	0.404	− 0.090	0.494	− 0.174	0.320
PWEL	0.243	− 1.224	1.467	− 1.275	0.192
SANT	2.224	− 1.761	3.985	− 2.228	1.757
PSER	16.500	4.028	12.472	0.565	13.037
TUTL	4.974	3.728	1.246	2.684	3.930
TCAP	8.938	0.636	8.302	− 1.240	7.062
TEXP	39.067	5.032	34.099	− 3.232	30.867

prior year data. Outside revenues were higher than estimated while own revenues were much smaller. Total expenditures were smaller than the pro forma budget but were higher than the norm for the same level of revenue. Education, welfare, sanitation and capital expenditures were higher than the expected norm. Fire, police, highways, and utility expenditures were less than the group norm budget estimates.

Appendix B shows the achieved results relative to average results for other Group 1 cities. Again, the revenue picture is rather bleak in that expenditures are higher than average and larger than revenues. The comparison of Cases C and D illustrates dramatically

TABLE 5-7

Case E — Budget Evaluation
(Numbers in thousands)

Ratio	Prior Year Pro Forma Budget	Variance	Actual Results	Variance	Prior Year Flexible Budget
PTAX	23.588	−5.128	18.460	0.109	18.351
OWNR	58.664	−19.862	38.802	−6.837	45.639
OUTR	17.921	2.858	20.779	6.837	13.942
TREV	76.585	−17.004	59.581	0.000	59.581
EDUC	7.582	7.582	0.000	5.899	5.899
FADM	1.838	0.286	1.552	−0.122	1.430
FIRE	6.663	1.446	5.217	−0.033	5.184
GCON	2.834	−0.084	2.918	−0.714	2.204
HOSP	0.919	0.919	0.000	0.715	0.715
HIGH	5.284	1.651	3.633	0.478	4.111
HOUS	0.536	0.403	0.133	0.284	0.417
INTR	2.527	1.186	1.341	0.625	1.966
PARK	0.306	0.306	0.000	0.238	0.238
RECR	3.676	1.852	1.824	1.036	2.860
POLC	10.569	2.380	8.189	0.033	8.222
PBLD	1.072	0.360	0.712	0.122	0.834
PWEL	0.383	0.383	0.000	0.298	0.298
SANT	5.744	−0.086	5.830	−1.361	4.469
PSER	37.603	14.095	23.508	5.746	29.254
TUTL	8.424	3.101	5.323	1.231	6.554
TCAP	16.083	9.248	6.835	5.677	12.512
TEXP	82.023	34.858	47.165	16.646	63.811

different financial patterns between two low income, low growth cities. One appears to be accommodating its fiscal activities to its situation by tailoring service levels to available resources. The other city appears to be experiencing severe fiscal stress.

Contrasting High and Low Growth

Tables 5-7 and 5-8 provide another comparison, this time between high and low growth as experienced by high income cities. Case E concerns a Group 2 (high income, low growth) city while

TABLE 5-8

Case F — Budget Evaluation
(Numbers in thousands)

Ratio	Prior Year Group Norm Budget	Policy Variances	Actual Results	Performance Variances	Prior Year Flexible Budget
PTAX	4.634	−0.226	4.408	−0.075	4.483
OWNR	15.035	4.141	19.176	4.631	14.545
OUTR	5.561	−4.813	0.748	−4.631	5.379
TREV	20.596	−0.672	19.924	0.000	19.924
EDUC	0.886	0.886	0.000	0.857	0.857
FADM	0.371	−0.382	0.753	−0.394	0.359
FIRE	1.298	−0.549	1.847	−0.592	1.255
GCON	0.618	−0.048	0.666	−0.068	0.598
HOSP	0.247	0.033	0.214	0.025	0.239
HIGH	1.174	−0.428	1.602	−0.466	1.136
HOUS	0.309	0.309	0.000	0.299	0.299
INTR	0.721	−0.331	1.052	−0.355	0.697
PARK	0.062	−0.028	0.090	−0.030	0.060
RECR	0.947	0.003	0.944	−0.027	0.917
POLC	2.307	−0.473	2.780	−0.549	2.231
PBLD	0.247	0.021	0.226	0.013	0.239
PWEL	0.144	0.144	0.000	0.139	0.139
SANT	1.339	0.029	1.310	−0.015	1.295
PSER	7.662	−0.196	7.858	−0.446	7.412
TUTL	2.698	−2.788	5.486	−2.876	2.610
TCAP	4.943	3.165	1.778	3.004	4.782
TEXP	19.505	−1.726	21.231	−2.363	18.868

Case F concerns a Group 4 (high income, high growth) city. City E experienced a dramatic decline in revenues, relative to the expected norm based upon prior period estimates, as indicated in Table 5-7. In this respect, it is similar to the city described in Case D. Property taxes in City E, however, were approximately equal to the expected norm and total expenditures were considerably less than the expected norm. Only sanitation expenditures exceeded the norm by large amounts. On the other hand, most of the expenditures were below the norm. Personal service expenditures and capital expenditures were considerably below the expected norm.

A similar pattern is found in Appendix C by a comparison between actual results and average group results. Property taxes were higher than the average for a Group 2 city with the same total revenue, however, most expenditures were below the norm. Case E is an example of a fiscally strained city that appears to be dealing with its fiscal problems by holding down expenditures.

Case F is a Group 4 (high income, high growth) city that is not growing at the group norm rate. Table 5-8 reveals that expected revenues based on group norms were greater than actual. The city had higher than expected own revenue and total expenditures. Variances generally revealed that expenditures exceeded group norms, and this pattern is also reflected in Appendix D. Fire, highways, police, interest, personal services, and utilities expenditures were well above the norm, and both total revenue and total expenditures exceeded the norms. Case F illustrates a city that appears to be prosperous but has not controlled expenditures to keep them in line with available resources.

Thus, in comparison, Case E is a low growth city that has dealt with its fiscal constraints while Case F is a high growth community that has not kept services in line with resources. A relatively wealthy city can suffer fiscal strain just as a poorer community if financial management is lax.

The comparison points out one of the values of this study's type of analyses: Financial problems do not have to arise as a result of a lack of wealth or slow growth. What is important is how a city responds to its resource constraints. Comparing cities to other similar cities, where similarities are based upon socio-demographic characteristics, can be helpful in pinpointing potential financial management problems that may plague a city of any wealth.

Appendix C

Case C — Performance Evaluation

(Numbers in thousands)

Ratio	Current Year Group Norm Budget	Policy Variances	Actual Results	Performance Variances	Current Year Flexible Budget
PTAX	12.382	−8.228	4.154	−9.574	13.728
OWNR	33.527	7.270	40.797	3.624	37.173
OUTR	17.426	1.729	15.697	−3.624	19.321
TREV	50.953	5.541	56.494	0.000	56.494
EDUC	5.860	5.860	0.000	6.497	6.497
FADM	0.917	0.100	0.817	0.200	1.017
FIRE	3.669	−1.345	5.014	−0.946	4.068
GCON	1.376	0.009	1.367	0.158	1.525
HOSP	0.917	0.729	0.188	0.829	1.017
HIGH	2.599	−0.675	3.274	−0.393	2.881
HOUS	0.968	−0.233	1.201	−0.128	1.073
INTR	1.478	−5.923	7.401	−5.763	1.638
PARK	0.153	−0.034	0.187	−0.018	0.169
RECR	1.630	−0.455	2.085	−0.277	1.808
POLC	4.841	−2.275	7.16	−1.749	5.367
PBLD	0.560	−1.016	1.576	−0.955	0.621
PWEL	0.306	0.306	0.000	0.339	0.339
SANT	2.802	0.654	2.148	0.959	3.107
PSER	20.585	−1.250	21.835	0.989	22.824
TUTL	6.522	6.522	0.000	7.231	7.231
TCAP	10.191	−4.224	14.415	−3.116	11.299
TEXP	48.711	−1.659	50.370	3.638	54.008

Appendix D

Case D — Performance Evaluation

(Numbers in thousands)

Ratio	Current Year Group Norm Budget	Policy Variances	Actual Results	Performance Variances	Current Year Flexible Budget
PTAX	9.480	0.603	10.083	2.318	7.765
OWNR	25.670	−10.807	14.863	−6.162	21.025
OUTR	13.342	3.748	17.090	6.162	10.928
TREV	39.012	−7.059	31.953	0.000	31.953
EDUC	4.486	−3.358	7.844	−4.169	3.675
FADM	0.702	0.039	0.663	−0.088	0.575
FIRE	2.809	1.339	1.470	0.831	2.301
GCON	1.053	0.133	0.920	−0.057	0.863
HOSP	0.702	0.104	0.598	−0.023	0.575
HIGH	1.990	1.079	0.911	0.719	1.630
HOUS	0.741	0.280	0.461	0.146	0.607
INTR	1.131	0.462	0.669	0.258	0.927
PARK	0.117	−0.055	0.172	−0.076	0.096
RECR	1.248	−0.260	1.508	−0.486	1.022
POLC	3.706	1.790	1.916	1.120	3.036
PBLD	0.429	−0.065	0.494	−0.143	0.351
PWEL	0.234	−1.233	1.467	−1.275	0.192
SANT	2.146	−1.839	3.985	−2.228	1.757
PSER	15.761	3.289	12.472	0.437	12.909
TUTL	4.994	3.748	1.246	2.844	4.090
TCAP	7.803	−0.499	8.302	−1.911	6.391
TEXP	37.296	3.197	34.099	−3.552	30.547

Appendix E

Case E — Performance Evaluation

(Numbers in thousands)

Ratio	Current Year Pro Forma Budget	Variance	Actual Results	Variance	Current Year Flexible Budget
PTAX	19.484	−1.024	18.460	1.777	16.683
OWNR	52.956	−14.154	38.802	−6.539	45.341
OUTR	16.631	4.148	20.779	6.539	14.240
TREV	69.587	−10.006	59.581	0.000	59.581
EDUC	3.619	3.619	0.000	2.098	3.098
FADM	1.531	−0.021	1.552	−0.241	1.311
FIRE	5.706	0.489	5.217	−0.331	4.886
GCON	2.505	−0.413	2.918	−0.773	2.145
HOSP	0.696	0.696	0.000	0.596	0.596
HIGH	4.732	1.099	3.633	0.419	4.052
HOUS	0.765	0.632	0.133	0.522	0.655
INTR	2.157	0.816	1.341	0.506	1.847
PARK	0.278	0.278	0.000	0.238	0.238
RECR	3.131	1.307	1.824	0.857	2.681
POLC	9.325	1.136	8.189	−0.205	7.984
PBLD	0.905	0.193	0.712	0.063	0.775
PWEL	0.209	0.209	0.000	0.179	0.179
SANT	5.080	−0.750	5.830	−1.481	4.349
PSER	29.435	5.927	23.508	1.695	25.203
TUTL	7.585	2.262	5.323	1.171	6.494
TCAP	12.526	5.691	6.835	3.890	10.725
TEXP	67.500	20.335	47.165	10.629	57.794

Appendix F

Case F — Performance Evaluation
(Numbers in thousands)

Ratio	Current Year Group Norm Budget	Policy Variances	Actual Results	Performance Variances	Current Year Flexible Budget
PTAX	3.947	0.461	4.408	0.304	4.104
OWNR	14.159	5.017	19.176	4.452	14.724
OUTR	5.001	−4.253	0.748	−4.452	5.200
TREV	19.160	0.760	19.924	0.000	19.924
EDUC	0.862	0.862	0.000	0.897	0.897
FADM	0.364	−0.389	0.753	−0.374	0.379
FIRE	1.207	−0.604	1.847	−0.592	1.255
GCON	0.594	−0.072	0.666	−0.048	0.618
HOSP	0.192	−0.022	0.214	−0.015	0.199
HIGH	1.111	−0.491	1.602	−0.446	1.156
HOUS	0.192	0.192	0.000	0.199	0.199
INTR	0.728	−0.324	1.052	−0.295	0.757
PARK	0.057	−0.033	0.090	−0.030	0.060
RECR	0.881	−0.063	0.944	−0.027	0.917
POLC	2.165	−0.615	2.780	−0.529	2.251
PBLD	0.211	−0.015	0.226	−0.007	0.219
PWEL	0.134	0.134	0.000	0.139	0.139
SANT	1.341	0.031	1.310	0.085	1.395
PSER	7.300	−0.558	7.858	−0.267	7.591
TUTL	2.586	−2.900	5.486	−2.796	2.690
TCAP	4.311	2.533	1.778	2.705	4.483
TEXP	18.240	−2.991	21.231	−2.263	18.968

Selected Bibliography

Surveys

Bahl, R. and L. Schroeder, *Forecasting Local Governments' Budgets* (Syracuse University, 1979).

Demoville, W. "Capital Budgeting in Municipalities," *Management Accounting* (July 1977), pp. 17-20.

Fisher, G. "Interstate Variation in State and Local Government Expenditures," *National Tax Journal* (March 1964), pp. 55-74.

Granof, M. "Financial Forecasting in Municipalities: How Accurate?" *Government Accountants Journal* (Winter 1977-78), pp. 18-25.

Moore, P. "Types of Budgeting and Budgeting Problems in American Cities," *International Journal of Public Administration* (1980), pp. 501-514.

Moore, P. "Zero-Base Budgeting in American Cities," *Public Administration Review* (May/June 1980), pp. 253-258.

Multi-year Revenue and Expenditure Forecasting (U.S. Department of Housing and Urban Development, 1980).

Scot, C. *Forecasting Local Government Spending* (Urban Institute, 1972).

Skelcher, C. "From Programme Budgeting to Policy Analysis: Corporate Approaches in Local Government," *Public Administration* (Summer 1980), pp. 155-172.

Trends in the Fiscal Condition of Cities: 1978-1980 (U.S. Government Printing Office, 1980).

Vanderbilt, D. "Budgeting in Local Government: Where Are We Now," *Public Administration Review* (Sept./Oct. 1977), pp. 538-542.

Williams, D. and D. Harris, "Corporate Management and Planning in Local Government," *Long Range Planning* (August 1976), pp. 46-51.

Manuals

Chang, S. and P. Kelly, *Ten Year Economic and Revenue Forecasting and Alternative Fiscal Plans for Mobile.*

City of Dallas Long-Range Financial Plan 1978-83 (1970).

The City of New York Financial Plan: Fiscal Years 1979-1983 (1979).

City of San Antonio, Long Range Financial Forecast 1979-84 (1979).
Five Year Projection, 1978-79 through 1982-83 (City of Portland, Oregon, 1977).
Madere, L. *Municipal Budget Projections, Econometric Revenue Forecasting* (1977).

Practical Guides

Babunakis, M. *Budgets: An Analytical and Procedural Handbook for Government and Nonprofit Organizations* (Greenwood Press, 1976).

Brett, P. "Budgetary Control," *Public Finance and Accountancy* (April 1976), pp. 118-119.

Caldwell, K. "Efficiency and Effectiveness Measurement in State and Local Government," *Governmental Finance* (November 1973), pp. 19-21.

Castello, A. "The Model Cities Program — An Application of PPBS," *Management Accounting* (January 1973), pp. 29-33.

Chang, S. "Municipal Revenue Forecasting," *Growth & Change* (October 1979), pp. 38-46.

Coppie, C. "The City: Management by Crisis or Crisis Management," *Management Accounting* (November 1978), pp. 13-21.

Cramer, R. "Local Government Expenditure Forecasting," *Governmental Finance* (November 1978), pp. 3-9.

Economic Analysis for Local Government (Municipal Finance Officers Association, 1978).

Flynn, J. "Municipal Budgeting: The Dilemma of Supply vs. Demand," *Touche Ross Tempo* (1979), pp. 41-43.

Galambos, E. and A. Schreiber, *Making Sense Out of Dollars: Economic Analysis for Local Government* (National League of Cities, 1978).

Groves, S., M. Godsey, and M. Shulman, "Financial Indicators for Local Government," *Public Budgeting and Finance* (Summer 1981), pp. 5-19.

Guy, R. "Budgeting: Program Budgeting for Smaller Governmental Units," *Governmental Finance* (August 1975).

Henderson, H. "Revenue Forecasting in a Working Perspective," *Governmental Finance* (November 1978), pp. 11-15.

Holder, W. and R. Ingram, "Flexible Budgeting and Standard Costing: Keys to Effective Cost Control," *Government Accountants Journal* (Fall 1976).

Ingram, R. and R. Copeland, *Local Government Financial Data File (LOGOFILE) An Introduction and Guide for Users* (University of South Carolina, 1982).

Javits, J. "The Need for Economic Planning," *Managerial Planning* (May-June 1976), pp. 1-3.

Jones, G. and D. Gabhart, "Danger, This City Is in Financial Trouble," *Management Accounting* (October 1979), pp. 19-22.

Kelly, J. "Allocation Criteria in Budgeting," *Governmental Finance* (August 1978), pp. 26-27.

Lawrence, C. "Study of a Program Budget for a Small City," *Journal of Accountancy* (November 1972), pp. 52-57.

Matson, M. "Capital Budgeting — Fiscal and Physical Planning," *Governmental Finance* (August 1976), pp. 42-48.

McBride, H. "Benefit-Cost Analysis and Local Government Decision-Making," *Governmental Finance* (February 1975), pp. 31-34.

Mercer, J. "Five-Year Operating Budget," *Governmental Finance* (February 1973), pp. 30-31.

Municipal Fiscal Indicators: An Information Bulletin of the Management, Finance and Personnel Task Force of the Urban Consortium (U.S. Dept. of Housing and Urban Development, 1980).

Petersen, J. "Simplification and Standardization of State and Local Government Fiscal Indicators," *National Tax Journal* (September 1977), pp. 299-311.

Phillips, J. "Framing an Operating Budget within the Local Economic Climate," *Governmental Finance* (May 1972), pp. 18-19.

Potthoff, E. "Pre-Planning for Budget Reductions," *Public Management* (March 1975), pp. 13-14.

Rosenberg, P. and W. Stallings, *Is Your City Heading for Financial Difficulty: A Guidebook for Small Cities and Other Governmental Units* (Municipal Finance Officers Association, 1978).

Simpson, C. "Municipal Budgeting — A Case of Priorities," *Governmental Finance* (August 1976), pp. 12-19.

Snyder, J., *Fiscal Management and Planning in Local Government* (Lexington Books, 1977).

Stallings, W. "Improve Budget Communications in Smaller Local Governments," *Governmental Finance* (August 1978), pp. 18-25.

Teeters, N. "Federal, State and Local Budgets," *Methods and Techniques of Business Forecasting* (1974), pp. 96-123.

Usher, C. and G. Cornia, "Goal Setting and Performance Assessment in Municipal Budgeting," *Public Administration Review* (March/April 1981), pp. 229-235.

Watkins, J. "Real Revenue Management in Local Government," *Governmental Finance* (August 1975), pp. 18-21.

White, M. "Budget Policy: Where Does It Begin and End?" *Governmental Finance* (August 1978), pp. 2-7.

Case Studies

Bahl, R. *Metropolitan City Expenditures: A Comparative Analysis.* (University of Kentucky Press, 1968).

Bahl, R., E. Cupoli and J. Liro, "Forecasting the Local Government Budget," *National Tax Association Proceedings* (November 1977).

Chang, S. "Forecasting Revenues to Municipal Government: The Case of Mobile, Alabama," *Governmental Finance* (February 1976), pp. 16-20.

Coppie, C. "Fiscal Planning for the Nation's Capital," *Management Accounting* (January 1978), pp. 39-48.

Hansen, E. "Municipal Finances in Perspective: A Look at Inter-Jurisdictional Spending and Revenue Patterns," *Studies on Measurement and Evaluation of the Economic Efficiency of Public and Private Nonprofit Institutions,* supplement to the *Journal of Accounting Research* (1977), pp. 156-162.

Homan, H., R. Broom, and J. Murray, "Therapy for an Ad Hoc Budget: The Case of Aurora, Colorado," *Governmental Finance* (August 1976), pp. 35-40.

Katz, H. "The Municipal Budgetary Response to Changing Labor Costs: The Case of San Francisco," *Industrial and Labor Relations Review* (July 1979), pp. 506-519.

McCaffery, J. "Revenue Budgeting: Dade County Tries a Decremental Approach," *Public Administration Review* (January 1981), pp. 179-189.

Muller, T. *Growing and Declining Urban Areas* (The Urban Institute, 1975).

"Municipal Accounting — A Better Blueprint Via IFMS," *Journal of Accountancy* (December 1976), pp. 42-52.

Singleton, D. and B. Smith, "Zero-Based Budgeting in Wilmington, Delaware," *Governmental Finance* (August 1976), pp. 20-29.

Theoretical Studies

Downs, A. "An Economic Theory of Political Action in a Democracy," *Journal of Political Economy* (1957), pp. 135-150.

Hirsch, W. *The Economics of State and Local Governments* (McGraw-Hill, 1970).

Litvack, J. and W. Oates, "Group Size and the Output of Public Goods: Theory and an Application to the State-Local Finance in the United States," *Public Finance* (1970), pp. 42-58.

Samuelson, P. "The Pure Theory of Public Expenditures," *Review of Economic and Statistics* (November 1954), pp. 87-89.

Tiebout, C. "A Pure Theory of Local Expenditures," *Journal of Political Economy* (August 1956), pp. 416-424.

Empirical Studies

Aronson, R. and E. Schwartz, "Financial Public Goods and the Distribution of Population in a System of Local Governments," *National Tax Journal* (June 1973), pp. 278-287.

Bahl, R. "Determinants of Changes in State and Local Government Expenditures," *National Tax Journal* (March 1965), pp. 47-50.

Bahl, R. "Intra-Urban Interactions, Social Structure, and Urban Government Expenditures: A Stochastic Model," *Social Economic Planning Sciences* (December 1969), pp. 279-290.

Bahl, R. and R. Saunders, "Factors Associated with Variation in State and Local Government Spending," *Journal of Finance* (September 1966), pp. 523-534.

Booth, D. "The Differential Impact of Manufacturing and Mercantile Activity on Local Government Expenditures and Revenues," *National Tax Journal* (March 1977), pp. 33-43.

Borcherding, T. and R. Deacon, "The Demand for the Services of Non-Federal Governments," *The American Economic Review* (December 1972), pp. 891-901.

Bradford, D. and H. Kelejian, "An Econometric Model of the Flight to the Suburbs," *Journal of Political Economy* (May 1973), pp. 566-589.

Cebula, R. "Interstate Migration and the Tiebout Hypothesis: An Analysis According to Race, Sex, and Age," *Journal of the American Statistical Association* (December 1974), pp. 876-879.

Clark, T. "Fiscal Management of American Cities: Funds Flow Indicators," *Studies on Measurement and Evaluation of the Economic Efficiency of Public and Private Nonprofit Institutions,* supplement to the *Journal of Accounting Research* (1977), pp. 54-94.

Clark, T. "Community Social Indicators: From Analytical Models to Policy Applications," *Urban Affairs Quarterly* (September 1973), pp. 3-36.

Davis, O. and G. Haines, "A Political Approach to a Theory of Public Expenditures," *National Tax Journal* (September 1966), pp. 259-275.

Dye, T. *Politics, Economics, and the Public: Policy Outcomes in the American States* (Chicago: Rand, McNally, 1966).

Fisher, G. "Determinants of State and Local Government Expenditures: A Preliminary Analysis," *National Tax Journal* (December 1961), pp. 349-352.

Fisher, R. "Local Sales Taxes: Tax Rate Differentials, Sales Loss, and Revenue Estimation," *Public Finance Quarterly* (April 1980), pp. 171-188.

Friedman, L. "Control, Management, and Planning — An Empirical Examination," *Public Administration Review* (November/December 1975), pp. 625-628.

Greytak, D., R. Gistely, and R. Dinkelmeyer, "The Effects of Inflation on Local Government Expenditures," *National Tax Journal* (December 1974), pp. 583-593.

Ingram, R. and R. Copeland, "Municipal Accounting Information and Voting Behavior," *The Accounting Review* (October 1981).

Klay, W. "Budgeting and Rapid Local Growth," *Southern Review of Public Administration* (December 1977), pp. 303-314.

Ladd, H. "Municipal Expenditure and the Rate of Population Change," (working paper, Harvard University, May 1979).

Leone, R. "The Fiscal Decline of Older Cities: Causes and Cures," *National Tax Journal* (September 1976), pp. 257-260.

McCaffery, J. and J. Bowman, "Participatory Democracy and Budgeting: The Effects of Proposition 13," *Public Administration Review*, (November/December 1978), pp. 530-538.

Mikesell, J. "Property Tax Assessment Practice and Income Elasticities," *Public Finance Quarterly* (January 1978), pp. 53-65.

Miller, S. and W. Tabb, "A New Look at a Pure Theory of Local Expenditures," *National Tax Journal* (June 1973), pp. 161-76.

Minge, D. "Law as a Determinant of Resource Allocation by Local Government," *National Tax Journal* (December 1977), pp. 399-410.

Nathan, R. and C. Adams, "Undertaking Central City Hardship," *Political Science Quarterly* (Spring 1976), pp. 47-62.

Oates, W. "The Effect of Property Taxes and Local Public Spending on Property Values: An Empirical Study of Tax Capitalization and the Tiebout Hypothesis," *Journal of Political Economy* (November 1969), pp. 957-971.

Ohls, J. and T. Wales, "Supply and Demand for State and Local Services," *The Review of Economics and Statistics*, pp. 424-430.

Pogue, T. and L. Sgontz, "Factors Influencing State-Local Spending: An Extension of Recent Empirical Investigations," *Mississippi Valley Journal of Business and Economics* (Fall 1968), pp. 72-82.

Reschovsky, A. "Residential Choice and the Local Public Sector: An Alternative Test of the 'Tiebout Hypothesis'," *Journal of Urban Studies* (1979), pp. 501-519.

Sachs, S. and R. Harris, "The Determinants of State and Local Government Expenditures and Intergovernmental Flow of Funds," *National Tax Journal* (March 1964), pp. 75-85.

Stamm, C. and J. Howell, *Urban Fiscal Stress: A Comparative Analysis of Sixty-six U.S. Cities* (Touche Ross and Co., 1979).

Weicher, J. and R. Emerine, "Econometric Analysis of State and Local Aggregate Expenditure Functions," *Public Finance* (1973), pp. 69-83.

Zimmerman, J. "The Municipal Accounting Maze: An Analysis of Political Incentives," *Studies of Measurement and Evaluation of the Economic Efficiency of Public and Private Nonprofit Institutions*, supplement to the *Journal of Accounting Research* (1977), pp. 107-144.

National Association of Accountants Committee on Research 1983-1984

Donald W. Baker
Chairman
Southwire Company
Carrollton, Georgia

George Bannon
Moravian College
Bethlehem, Pennsylvania

Robert U. Boehman
Jasper Rubber Products
Jasper, Indiana

James Colford
IBM Corporation
White Plains, New York

James L. Crandall
Chicago, Illinois

Willard Cox
Oil City Iron Works
Corsicana, Texas

Dennis C. Daly
University of Minnesota
Minneapolis, Minnesota

Patricia P. Douglas
University of Montana
Missoula, Montana

Margaret Duffy
Arthur Andersen & Co.
New York, New York

James Don Edwards
University of Georgia
Athens, Georgia

Charles L. Grant
Becton Dickinson
  Laboratory System
Parsippany, New Jersey

Wallis W. Grissett
Pensacola, Florida

Robert E. Hampel
Keller-Crescent Co.
Evansville, Indiana

Neil E. Holmes
The Marley Company
Mission, Kansas

John H. Holzapfel
Coopers & Lybrand
Pittsburgh, Pennsylvania

James O. Ingle
Ingle, White & Co.
Atlanta, Georgia

Charles D. Mecimore
University of North Carolina
Greensboro, North Carolina

Larry E. Newman
Ernst & Whinney
Birmingham, Alabama

John A. O'Connor
Fesco Plastics Corp.
Kankakee, Illinois

John B. Pollara
Zieman Manufacturing Co.
Whittier, California

Leroy H. Rogero, Jr.
Touche Ross & Co.
Dayton, Ohio

Mildred B. Stephens
Educational Testing Service
Princeton, New Jersey

Stanley P. Vroman
Prince Gardner
St. Louis, Missouri

Thomas H. Williams
University of Wisconsin
Madison, Wisconsin